# *Natural Choices for Attention Deficit Disorder*

# Natural Choices for Attention Deficit Disorder

## For Adults and Children Who Want to Achieve Mental Clarity

by:
**Jane Oelke, N.D., Ph.D.**

Publisher:
Natural Choices, Inc.
Stevensville, Michigan
www.NaturalChoicesForYou.com

"Happy Harry" illustrated by: Jessica Oelke

Printed in the United States of America
by Patterson Printing, Benton Harbor, MI

Publisher:  Natural Choices, Inc.
Other book in print: *Natural Choices for Fibromyalgia*

ISBN 0-9715512-1-9

Library of Congress Control Number 2005

# *Acknowledgements*

Research and development for the content of this book has come from many experiences with clients who have been diagnose with Attention Deficit Disorder, or believe they have the symptoms, or who just want to remember and think more clearly. These clients, both young and old, have helped me understand and explain to others these natural choices that can truly help other people feel better.

Also I would like to acknowledge Robert Waldon, a friend and educator who taught me about the learning patterns and brain exercises explained in Section 4. His teaching style has helped me explain these exercises to others in my own presentations.

And I would like to acknowledge my family and colleagues who continue to support me in my endeavor to do presentations and consultations to assist people on how to be healthier naturally.

# Natural Choices For Attention Deficit Disorder

## Table of Contents

# Section 1

# Defining Attention Deficit Disorder

# *Defining Attention Deficit Disorder*

## Quick Find Outline

# What is Attention Deficit Disorder?

Each one of us has experienced days in our life where we do not want to pay attention, tend to lose things, forget what we are supposed to do next, or have excess energy or stress that needs to be released. Yet, when these times of inattention, impulsiveness, or hyperactivity affect how successful we are in our daily life then we have to look at the underlying cause.

Attention Deficit Disorder (ADD), also commonly called Attention Deficit Hyperactivity Disorder (ADHD) was officially defined in the early 1990's as "a disorder of inattention, hyperactivity, and impulsivity that presents early in life." At first it was thought to be genetic in nature, and the diagnosis would come after looking for a family history of hyperactivity or other psychological disorders that cause similar symptoms. Some medical professionals do not believe it is a real disorder, just an excuse for unorganized or unruly behavior. Yet now ADD has been officially diagnosed in 12% of children and 4% of adults, and the numbers continue to grow, as people understand more about their mental and physical health.

The symptoms related to Attention Deficit Disorder do affect the lives of both children and adults. The causes of Attention Deficit Disorder symptoms are varied. Very few people who have been diagnosed have a history of any psychological disorder. Other factors are now becoming evident that can cause many of the symptoms of ADD.

From personal experience, I have seen small changes in diet and exercise make enormous shifts in behaviors. But there is not just one answer for everyone. Take a real look at your current situation. Are you the one with Attention Deficit Disorder? Or is it one of your adult family members or children? What are the behaviors you are concerned about? What role do you play in creating the person's lifestyle, and how does their behavior affect yours? For example, it is amazing to me to see parents trying to control their children's imaginations to suit their own experiences. I hope to share some specific examples for you to learn from in the following sections.

## **Focus of This Book**

The way our brain cells communicate is affected by our lifestyle, including our diet, our sleep patterns, and our reaction to stress in our lives. In the following chapters we will look at Attention Deficit Disorder and answer some questions. Is it a real problem or a truly misdiagnosed disorder that is coming from our current lifestyles? Are there environmental factors that can affect or cause our nervous system to react differently? We will look at various areas of health and lifestyle that do affect our moods, our behavior, our energy levels, and our thinking ability. And we will look at Attention Deficit behavior in children and adults since many more adults are now realizing that they have good reasons for their nervous energy, lack of concentration, or difficulty remembering names and what they read.

We will take a look at the variety of symptoms related to ADD in children and adults, and how they are grouped and scored to become "officially" ADD or ADHD. We all have a few of these symptoms at some time in our life, but how they affect our work and relationships is the key to understanding if ADD can truly be an identified cause of these symptoms.

We will also consider the role of neurotransmitters, or brain chemicals that help our brain cells communicate effectively. When there is a deficiency of the neurotransmitter dopamine we can become more impulsive, and have less self-control. When the neurotransmitter norepinephrine is low, hyperactivity symptoms occur. Too much serotonin can cause aggression, and too little serotonin can cause depression. So a balance of neurotransmitters is very important.

Our diet affects our behavior, and we will discuss how foods can cause our brain chemicals to go out of balance. Environmental chemicals, preservatives, and food allergies are also factors, especially seen in children. We will discover specific ways to keep the blood sugar in balance to avoid the brain fog associated with low blood sugar. Also we will pay attention to the importance of getting certain nutrients daily to balance the nervous system and brain chemistry.

Personality and learning patterns, including inherited traits, can affect how we deal with stress in our lives. We will look at homeopathic personality profiles and how to use homeopathic remedies to reduce stresses that have built up causing ADD symptoms. We will also look at learning patterns, and movement exercises that can improve learning and thinking ability.

Once a child has been labeled as ADD, the parents, teachers, and administrators are often satisfied that they are not responsible for the problems that they have had with that child. Yet, now begins the real assignment. How can we effectively help this child become a successful adult? What are the avenues to look at? Does daily nutrition affect their behavior? Do they have specific learning patterns that can be encouraged to help them learn more effectively? Are there natural remedies that will help them with their behaviors?

A Quick Find Outline is located at the beginning of each of the four sections. This outline is designed to help you find the specific information you are looking for. A list of each major topic in that section is listed along with the page number where it first appears.

## Attention Deficit Disorder Defined

Attention Deficit Disorder has been classified as a condition based on a persistent pattern of one to three major symptoms. They are:

- **Inattention** includes being distracted easily, disorganized and careless. Inattentive people have excessive accidents or errors, lose things easily, and cannot stay focused on any one task. They tend to daydream and have trouble concentrating or remembering to do a sequence of actions in the assigned order.

- **Hyperactivity** includes having nervous energy, racing thoughts, and obsessive-compulsive behaviors. These people are in constant motion, even when sitting they will have to fidget with their hands or feet, or twist around in their chair.

- **Impulsivity** includes acting before thinking about the consequences. Impulsive people will say or do whatever comes into their mind at the moment. They may consider themselves spontaneous, but others view them as reckless and irresponsible.

There is some question about Attention Deficit Disorder being a real disorder, or one caused by the environment. Studies show many causes of attention difficulties and thinking problems. Hyperactivity is not always a symptom in everyone having attention deficit disorder, and can be considered a totally separate condition.

Yet, Attention Deficit Hyperactivity Disorder (ADHD) has become a common diagnosis for many school age children today. It affects about three times more boys than girls, and it may be combined with other psychological disorders such as obsessive-compulsive disorder or depression.

Some researchers say that a child will grow out of Attention Deficit Hyperactivity Disorder by the time they are adults. Yet many adults are now realizing that they have symptoms that are slightly different than those listed for children. They may have trouble organizing or planning their lives, have a chronically messy environment, may always be late, and are easily overwhelmed by daily living tasks. They many have poor financial management, unable to pay bills on time because of poor budgeting of income. They will change from one interest to another, having trouble really knowing what is important to them.

If you are an adult believing that you have Attention Deficit Disorder, look at your specific symptoms. Do you have problems with focus and concentration that are affecting your career? Are you more intuitive or creative than your job allows, creating distractions. When necessary are you able to intensely focus easily on your own interests. Are you better as your own boss? Or are you too distractible to set your own schedule? Do you like to try new creative approaches to old traditions?

### How is it treated?

Stimulants drugs are the most common treatment recommended for ADD or ADHD. In the April 24, 2000 issue of Newsweek there was an article called "Does My Child Need Ritalin? The challenge is to use them wisely." The School of Medicine at John Hopkins University estimates that over one million children use Ritalin daily. And other prescription drugs are commonly used when Ritalin does not help.

Even though the first treatment for ADD or ADHD is a pharmaceutical medication to control behavior, this should be done after a doctor rules out any other potential physical disorder such as blood sugar imbalances, allergies, thyroid dysfunction, or infection. Behavioral therapy should be used as an adjunct to any medications that are recommended, but are often overlooked while looking for a quick fix.

At this time there are a number of medications commonly prescribed for ADHD. The most common type of drug used is a stimulant. This includes Ritalin, the most commonly used prescription drug for ADHD. Stimulants are only meant to be used for a short time, not longer than 12 to 14 months. Stimulants tend to help reduce the symptoms of ADHD in many children. Ritalin can cause side effects such as insomnia, headaches, anxiety, nausea, appetite loss, growth retardation and compulsive behaviors. A large percentage of children become robotic, lethargic, depressed, or withdrawn on stimulants. In 1995, more than 6 million prescriptions were being written every year for Americans under the age of 18. And in 1996, the World Health Organization estimated that nearly 5 percent of all elementary schoolchildren in the United States were on Ritalin.

Other stimulant medications besides Ritalin used for ADHD are Adderall, Concerta, and Dexedrine. Adderall and Concerta are longer acting stimulants and so do not need to be taken as often as Ritalin. These stimulant medications work to increase the activity of the neurotransmitter dopamine in the brain. The common benefits of stimulant drugs are less distraction and a better ability to focus on tasks. Hyperactive children can now follow rules better and are easier to manage. They become less aggressive and more docile. These stimulant drugs do not enhance their learning ability other than to help them focus better.

Antidepressants are another class of drugs that are used to treat ADD when depressive symptoms are found and stimulants do not work well. One of the non-stimulant drugs that have been recently introduced is Strattera that affects the neurotransmitters differently than stimulants. Other medications that were originally created for other uses are now being prescribed to see if they can make a difference.

Strattera was introduced in 2003 as a non-stimulant medication that increases the activity of the neurotransmitter norepinephrine. Strattera is now the most common medication recommended for adult ADD. Some of the side effects of Strattera are dizziness due to a fall in blood pressure, dry mouth, abdominal pain, irritability and sleeping disturbances. Recently liver imbalances were being found with long-term use of Strattera, so consistent evaluation of symptoms and side effects are necessary.

The problem with trying too many medications is that their interaction has to be evaluated closely. I had a young client come in who was acting excessively irritable and aggressive. She had a new medication added to her stimulant medication and the combination of the two was making her have these unmanageable symptoms. Soon after she stopped the second medication her symptoms improved.

Stimulants and other medications can decrease the inattention, hyperactive, and impulsive symptoms related to Attention Deficit Disorder. Yet the effects of these medications should be evaluated regularly and adjusted as needed. Often when none of the medications work well, then underlying physical or mental conditions have to be discovered. Even with medications, other avenues such as diet, allergies, nutritional supplementation, homeopathic remedies, and behavioral therapy should also be considered. When problems in these areas are solved they can assist the medication to work more effectively, or may shorten the time the medication is necessary.

# Symptoms and Personality Profiles

## Symptoms of Attention Deficit Disorder

The symptoms of Attention Deficit Disorder vary from person to person. Some people have hyperactive symptoms such as aggressive, restless, or uncontrollable behaviors that tend to cause difficulties at school or work situations. Others are slow learners and inattentive, who cannot follow directions or make decisions, and are often classified as daydreamers. Then there are some who become diagnosed with Attention Deficit Disorder because their creative minds are always looking for new ways of doing tasks, and so do not do well in structured settings either in school or at home.

In children, Attention Deficit Hyperactivity Disorder is usually diagnosed early in life, between the ages of 3 and 5 depending on the level of structured preschool activities. It often takes a specific event to get the parents to realize that they may have a child with ADD or ADHD. When they become too hard to handle, disrupt class, or talk back to authorities, it makes the parents realize that their child should be evaluated. Also if a child is so shy or sensitive that they do not talk to other adults or children, and cannot handle simple tasks, then the parents become concerned. Medical professionals use different questionnaires to evaluate children's symptoms. When evaluating a questionnaire make sure it includes your child's symptoms.

A good diagnosis looks at the number of symptoms the child has, how long they have had them, and the severity of the symptoms. The list below is divided into the three categories of **Attention Deficit Disorder symptoms for children**. To be "officially" diagnosed, at least 6 symptoms from the inattention category, and 6 symptoms from the hyperactive or impulsive categories have to be present. Then they have to have had them for at least 6 months, to the point where they have caused an obstruction in learning. or physical or mental development.

**Inattention** includes
- Being able to do only one task at a time
- Being reckless, making many mistakes on tasks to get them done quickly
- Extreme distractibility
- Daydreaming, not paying attention to others
- Lack of concentration
- Moving from one task to another before finishing the first task,
- Tendency to disturb others, interrupting
- Not listening when spoken to
- Forgetfulness, losing things easily
- Trouble keeping things organized.

**Hyperactive** includes
- Always on the go, being driven, acting obsessed with activity
- Excessive talking
- Temper tantrums, not being able to control movements when upset
- Not being able to sit still for any length of time
- Restlessness, having nervous energy
- Head knocking or other compulsive behavior

- Fidgeting with hands or feet, or other objects,
- Needing to touch everything
- Running or climbing at inappropriate times
- Not being able to play quietly

**Impulsive** includes

- Acting without thinking
- Self-destructive behavior like biting nails, scratching skin, or pulling hair
- Not being able to take turns or wait in line
- Impatience with tasks, getting frustrated quickly
- Inability to finish tasks
- Always looking for something new and exciting to do, tired of the "old" way quickly
- Not being able to wait for something they want
- Clumsiness
- Becoming violent (hitting or biting another child) to get what they want, or
- Making comments without thinking

In looking over these symptoms, it is common to believe that just about any child can and often does experience many of these symptoms. Again it is the severity of these symptoms that end up causing harmful tendencies or developmental difficulties that lead to a true diagnosis. Some of these symptoms can be caused by specific learning disabilities, speech and hearing disorders, or sleep disturbances.

**In adults, the symptoms of Attention Deficit Disorder** are displayed on a different level than the child's symptoms. Adults are expected to follow schedules, organize their time, money, and environment, and act responsibly. When any of these behaviors are exceedingly difficult, then it is appropriate to look into more specific ADD symptoms.

In adults, the same three categories of behavior have additional symptoms, which are:

**Inattention**
⇒ Chronic procrastinating
⇒ Difficulty getting organized
⇒ Starting new projects without completion
⇒ A sense of under achievement - having trouble getting life together
⇒ Easy distracted – tending to drift away in a conversation or thought

**Hyperactive**
⇒ Nervous energy
⇒ Racing mind
⇒ Needless worrying or a sense of impending doom
⇒ Low tolerance for stress and otherwise ordinary problems
⇒ Tendencies toward addictive behavior

**Impulsive**
⇒ Speaking without thinking
⇒ Difficulty solving problems
⇒ Always late
⇒ Trouble managing money
⇒ Being bored easily when trying to follow directed protocols.

As you can see, Attention Deficit Symptoms cover a wide range of behaviors. Ranging from hyperactive uncontrollable actions, to a spacey daydream state, both affecting learning ability and daily life experiences. Some people are always on the go, shifting from one subject or action to another make it difficult for others to keep up or work with them. Complaints will come from parents and teachers when trying to work with hyperactive children. They cannot believe that they can focus on anything.

Some of these hyperactive children also act out, becoming physical with others, talking or making noises to be noticed. I remember one 4 year-old boy who came into my office. He had to touch everything. I have a stuffed flamingo in my office that he had to touch as soon as he saw it. He played with the toys, getting tired of them quickly and began looking for other "toys" to touch. He wanted to look through drawers and cupboards to find more things, all within the first 10 minutes. Then as soon as he realized that we were talking about him, he began to make noises, or single note sounds, to drown out what we were saying. The sounds became louder the longer we tried to talk and stopped when we quit talking. He was not allowed in preschool because he hit or bit other children to get their attention. In some ways it seemed at first that he just wanted his own attention. But after finding food allergies and using homeopathic remedies his actions changed immensely. He became much more calm and focused, did not have to touch everything, and actually answered questions asked of him instead of making sounds.

Other times I have had children come into the office, and sit quietly, refusing to look at me, and not answering questions by either the parent or me. They seem off in their own world, making it difficult to realize if they are actually hearing what I am saying. They seem to have trouble learning because they do not seem to be aware of their environment and they do not provide feedback.

Adults who believe they may have attention deficit disorder symptoms are often very creative and intuitive people. They have a certain level of aptitude that when directed effectively can bring out the genius in them. These are often the people that come up with the new designs that change old ways of doing things that at first are thought to be impossible. When they can present their ideas in an organized form then their intellectual brilliance can shine.

Also it is important not to judge others on their own symptoms. It is essential to figure out the true cause of the problem. For example when someone seems easily distractible, is it because they are bored with the current environment, or do they like to constantly monitor everything around them? Are these people able to intensely focus on a task when necessary?

When people seem to be poor planners is it because they are truly disorganized and impulsive, or are do they want to be open to new opportunities? Some people work better independently than in a controlled environment, and also the opposite can be true. Others need a controlled environment to direct them, otherwise their mind is unsure as to the next step.

We can judge others as impatient or self-driven, when they see themselves as results orientated. They need to have lists and goals that they are constantly striving for, and when others get in the way they can feel overlooked. Then some people are considered impulsive, or willing to take chances more than others, so it is again important to understand the level of the imbalance based on a set standard and not on your own judgment.

When there truly is a diagnosis of ADD or ADHD then it is important to look at the potential causes of these symptoms. Is there a reason they have problems thinking in certain situations? Are they acting violent for a reason? What is causing them to be so restless that they cannot sit still? Are they really daydreaming or are they using their creative mind to avoid being bored?

Diagnosis of depression or mood swings is often related to Attention Deficit Disorder when not accompanied with hyperactivity. Depression often is a result of excess anxiety that causes the body to want to shut down to protect itself from getting too overwhelmed. The mind does not want to deal with social situations until it is able to restore itself. When we discuss the role of neurotransmitters you will be able to see the connection between depressive symptoms and Attention Deficit Disorder.

Specific learning patterns or physical issues can cause many of these symptoms. Are they in pain or do they have allergies that are causing these symptoms? Are there learning patterns causing anxiety because they are not being handled? Is there a speech or vision weakness that they are compensating for? Are they dealing with blood sugar imbalances that cause them to have trouble paying attention? All of these questions will be discussed in the following sections.

## Personality Profiles

Every person is unique, and cannot always fit into the traditional environment. As our world changes and knowledge expands, creating awareness of diversity in thoughts and actions, it becomes more difficult to fit people into specific personality profiles. Many different personality tests exist that can help you learn about your specific talents and abilities. We will look at just a couple types of general personality profiles here.

Personality profiles affect how people think and learn. People who are consistently shy will seem like they are not as interested in classroom activities as the outgoing person. Daydreamers, who may actually be bored and thinking of creative ideas, are judged by their actions.

Also by looking to see if they are right-brain or left-brain thinkers will make a difference on their learning patterns. Right-brain thinkers tend to see the creative side of a problem versus the left-brain thinker who tends to think about the detailed side of the problem.

When looking at personalities, we can also look at the way we process information, often broken down into visual, auditory and kinesthetic patterns. We will be specifically discussing how to test these different patterns in the section on learning and movement. Here we will give a general discussion of how they affect attention deficit symptoms.

Some children that are labeled hyperactive may just have trouble learning in their current environment. Some gifted and talented children will become bored with simple structured learning styles and will act out just to get some excitement in their life. They may be multitaskers, where they are more aware of their surroundings even when they are focusing on the specific task. Whereas some people can only focus on one task at a time, like reading only in complete quiet with no noise in the background, others do better with a little background stimulant that helps them concentrate.

Some people remember what they read by visual awareness. Some remember what they read only by saying aloud or silently each word on the page. Others have trouble remembering unless they can make notes on paper while reading text. The person who remembers just by reading is a **visual learner**. They see something written down, or a picture, and it stays in their memory. Many pure visual learners have a photographic memory.

The **auditory learner** needs to hear the words in their mind to remember what they read. They will be seen reading more slowly, and sometimes moving their mouth to silently say each word in the text. With pictures they will develop their own internal explanation of the picture as they see it, and remember the explanation instead of the actual picture.

The **kinesthetic learner** uses the concept of touch or experience to learn well. They need to use a practical hands-on approach to learning. These are the students taking notes in class, or while reading they will tend to doodle or fidget. This motion of writing, doodling, or fidgeting helps them remember what they are learning or reading. These are the learners who learn better in labs, or on field trips, where a hands-on approach helps them experience the new concepts.

Schools are trying to cater to these learning styles. Colleges now have on-line courses, for the independent learner who can understand visual concepts on their own, and then explain in writing the concepts back to the professor without any discussion needed or hands-on class participation. Most classes have classroom settings where you get together with others and discuss the course content. This helps the auditory learner understand the concepts better. Then there are lab classes, or hands-on classes that help you create the concepts using art or drama to act out the concept. Many middle school and high school programs are trying to use the integrative approach, by combining the English with the Social Studies topic, and art or drama, so that all types of learners can benefit.

Many people with ADD are visual thinkers associated with right-brain thinking. They tend to be more intuitive yet also have good problem solving abilities. They have strong visual memories but poor verbal memories, and have trouble explaining their decisions. They may have poor handwriting or seem to be uncoordinated. They will have good spatial skills but will seem to understand what they hear or read in a different way than was meant. They are highly creative yet will have trouble organizing their thoughts to get their idea understood.

Of course, there are combinations of each learning type. Some people may have to see, and hear, and do, the concept before remembering it. You can evaluate your own style by realizing what type of learning environment you like. Do you learn better in classroom settings with discussion groups? Or do you find that you learn better on your own, the self-taught approach? Or do you find that you need to take an intangible concept and make it tangible before you can understand it?

Then there are the people who are visionaries versus detail oriented. In many school settings we try to get students to learn specific details before they understand how we use the information in daily life. For many people knowing how to use information is actually more important than remembering it. There are detail-orientated people that will be good accountants and planners, and then general visionary people who will create the ideas for the detailed people to figure out.

Some children rebel in school settings because they cannot understand why they are learning something, and until they are taught how they will use the information they will almost refuse to learn it. Others have a creative side in them that needs to come out. They are the idea producers who are needed to create many of the new concepts developed in our world today. When these children are allowed to make some choices about their learning activities, and to feel a sense of control over their learning processes, the results can be impressive. Finding out how people learn is very helpful in assisting them to understand new things. The last section of this book is about using left and right brain concepts in learning.

## Additional Personality Profiles

Different temperament tests are used to measure specific personalities, and find out if you are more prone to be observant or introspective, tough-minded or friendly, scheduling or probing, or extroverted or introverted. By taking a specific **temperament test developed by David Kiersey** you can find out more about your own temperament. The test is available online or in the book "Please Understand Me" by David Keirsey.

Many psychologists today use the Keirsey Temperament Scale to discover one of 16 different temperaments. Each temperament has it's own strengths and weaknesses and it is necessary for our society to have a combination of all of these temperaments so that we can have diversity. Yet, different learning patterns in a group setting can cause distractions. People within certain temperaments, especially the divergent thinkers, are more likely to be classified as ADD. For example, people who are extroverted, observant, friendly and probing often have trouble focusing on one task for any length of time but enjoy social, artistic or athletic aspects of school. They are classified as Performers by their combination of temperaments. They are easily distracted and cannot sit still for more than a few minutes. They like to be in motion, either roaming around the room, or tapping their finger on the desk, or foot on the floor. They have difficulty staying on schedule or complying with structure of any kind.

Other temperament combinations create different personalities. The four main temperaments that are then separated into the 16 specific temperaments are:

**Rationals** – This type of person is always expanding their own knowledge. They will continue to learn so that they can be more competent, with enough knowledge to control their environment.

**Idealists** – This type of person will always be trying to improve themselves. They value integrity and reliability in themselves and others. They like to help others improve their lives also.

**Guardians** – This type of person likes to belong. They are will seek out community or group situations to be with people. They are stable people who like tradition, and tend to be conservative and dependable.

**Artisans** – This type of person likes spontaneity and freedom in their life. They act on impulse, like to create and play, and do not like to be constrained.

Most people who have Attention Deficit Disorder are Artisans. These are the people who are not looking for restraint or control, but want freedom and fun. These are the people who are the Performers, we just explained that tend to have hyperactivity with attention deficit disorder. Other temperaments will be more introspective, and may consist of students that do not participate in class discussions easily, but like to belong to a group for support. As teachers or parents, it is good to recognize the different temperaments and be able to adjust to the various learning styles.

## Understanding Neurotransmitters

Physical chemicals made by our body affect how well our brain thinks. Our brain cells communicate with each other using neurotransmitters. The word "neurotransmitter" can be divided into two parts meaning nervous system and transmitter, signifying that these chemicals are used to transmit information in the nervous system. The main neurotransmitters that affect our thinking ability are dopamine, serotonin, norepinephrine, acetylcholine and GABA. An imbalance of any one of these neurotransmitters can cause symptoms of Attention Deficit Disorder seen as problems in thinking, learning and remembering. Neurotransmitters are chemicals that affect our level of happiness, drive and motivation, our mental alertness and ability to focus, our emotional stability, and our feelings toward others.

In your brain are ten billion brain cells called neurons. Between each brain cell are these neurotransmitters that transmit thoughts from one cell to another. Neurotransmitters are used to create your physical and mental nervous system responses, including your emotions, pain responses, and enthusiasm about life. During each 24-hour period different neurotransmitters are activated to help our nervous system respond productively. During the night, calming neurotransmitters are activated to help you sleep, settle down your nervous system, and help you relax. During the day other neurotransmitters are used to create energy, create excitement, and stimulate your brain. Other neurotransmitters are secreted when exercising, or to control pain responses. It is very important that all of the major neurotransmitters are present every day as needed, and be in balance chemically. When they are out of balance many mental, emotional, and physical symptoms occur.

There are "feel good" neurotransmitters that help you feel happy, motivated, positive, and energetic. When you do not have enough of these neurotransmitters you will have symptoms of depression, irritability, sleeplessness, anxiety or panic attacks, excess pain responses, changeable moods, no excitement for life, memory problems, and brain fog.

In children, when neurotransmitters are too low, they can have more symptoms of uncontrollable behavior, and more difficulty paying attention or focusing. When they are very low then there is a tendency toward violent behavior. When their levels are good they will think more clearly, sleep more soundly, be more positive, motivated and focused, and feel more relaxed and peaceful.

The main causes of neurotransmitter deficiencies are genetics, stress, and diet. Stress can come from small and large traumas, a lack of sleep, or chronic pain, and will lower brain communication, Neurotransmitters are rejuvenated during the first couple of hours of sleep when the sleep is deep enough. Diet affects neurotransmitters when not enough amino acids are processed from protein foods daily. Certain combinations of amino acids are used to make neurotransmitters. A list of common "feel good" neurotransmitters are:

• **Acetylcholine** affects your memory, alertness, appetite control, and sexual performance

• **Dopamine** affects your feelings of happiness and satisfaction, focus, coordination, and appetite control.

• **Endorphins** are mood enhancing, natural painkillers, and affect your level of happiness. This is the neurotransmitter that is increased with exercise and chocolate.

• **Norepinephrine,** made from adrenalin, helps you feel alert, motivated, and energetic. It helps with appetite control and sexual excitement, and counteracts depression.

- **Phenylethylmine** helps improve feelings of pleasure and passion. High levels of phenylethylmine are found in chocolate.

The most common inhibitory neurotransmitter is called **GABA (Gamma Amino Butyric Acid)**. It is used throughout the nervous system to reduce stress, anxiety, panic and pain. It helps you feel more calm, focused, and in control.

**Serotonin** is the neurotransmitter that is affected by hormone levels. It helps you sleep, relieves depression, reduces cravings, controls emotions of worry and anxiety and helps improves self-esteem. A deficiency in serotonin affects how your other neurotransmitters function, so it is the one that is most often treated with anti-depressive drugs. A more detailed overview of each neurotransmitter and its effects on symptoms of Attention Deficit Disorder is discussed in the next chapter.

# *Can Stress Cause Learning Difficulties?*

Stress can affect virtually any part of the body and produce physical, mental and emotional symptoms altering metabolism, weakening the immune system and impairing coordination and thinking ability. Stress comes in many forms in our daily lives. We get stress from relationships, from school or work situations, and from our own expectations. How we learn to deal with stress makes a huge difference in how healthy we are. Continual stress eventually wears out our body. Studies by the American Medical Association have shown stress to be a factor in over 75% of all illnesses today.

**Stress** is a reaction to a perceived threat. Our stress response helps us prepare mentally and physically to take protective action. These survival instincts are needed when we have real danger. Our muscle strength increases during stress by raising blood supply and oxygen to our muscles. Stress does not help us become more creative, or rational, or smarter. Chronic stress has a detrimental effect on our health. When we sense danger our **adrenal glands secrete adrenalin** that initiates the fight or flight stress response.

The adrenalin is secreted at nerve endings to stimulate the sympathetic nervous system. The sympathetic nervous system controls our muscles, including the heart muscle, and many of the glands that regulate our hormones. When the blood is directed to the muscles during stress, the brain and digestive system do not get what they need to function. Over time lack of blood supply can create attention problems along with digestive disorders. Under stress, electrolytes contained in the blood are dispersed throughout the body, reducing cell membrane potential in the nervous system. This makes us more hypersensitive, or alert to everything that is happening around us. This can increase the sensation of pain, making chronic pain worse. It can also make it more difficult to focus since too many stimuli are affecting us, so learning becomes more difficult.

Adrenalin takes a while to break down since the liver is in charge of detoxifying it out of the blood and nerve endings. This is why it takes time to settle down after nearly having a car accident, or seeing a dramatic movie. During stress, the adrenal glands also secrete glucocorticoids, including cortisol. **Cortisol** increases blood sugar so that more energy can get into the muscles when needed. Cortisol also constricts blood vessels, increasing blood pressure. Increased cortisol also is associated with diminished learning and memory as well as lowered focus and attention abilities.

Excess cortisol decreases metabolism of protein, muscle strength, and calcium absorption. It also affects the assimilation of insulin causing body fat to be distributed in different areas. The extremities lose fat and muscle while the abdomen and face become fatter. Cortisol also affects the blood pressure and can cause depression symptoms. And excess cortisol affects neurotransmitters that weaken memory.

Physically, our hormones react with neurotransmitters in stressful situations. The hypothalamus, a gland in the brain, sends out hormones to react with the pituitary and adrenals to keep the body in balance. Our nervous system attempts to control basic body functions such as sleep, hunger, thirst, and emotions with neurotransmitters. The hormones and neurotransmitters try to maintain a balanced condition, using symptoms as signals that we are out of balance, often due to stress.

Stress comes from our perceptions, our mental and emotional responses to life experiences. Stress happens when our perceptions don't meet our expectations and we don't manage our reactions. We can't change events but we can change our perceptions. Stressful symptoms include feeling rushed, bored, depressed, irritated, frustrated, anxious, short-tempered, angered, unloved, unfulfilled, and disheartened. Any of these mental and emotional symptoms are feedback to you that hormones and neurotransmitters are out of balance. When you shift your perceptions you can affect your stress reactions, thereby changing many of your physical and emotional symptoms.

### Recognizing ADD and Stress Responses

Not all children who are overly energetic or particularly curious have Attention Deficit Hyperactivity Disorder. Neither do all busy, disorganized adults have ADD. What classifies real ADD over just being too busy is a high level of frustration. Adults and children with ADD are overly impatient to get things done, and are totally overwhelmed with anything in the environment. The whole world is too loud, too bright, too fast for them. They cannot filter out background noise, and so are affected by everything going on around them.

Many parents do not believe their child can be stressed. But children, especially infants, are highly sensitive to the emotions of their parents and caregivers. They sense fear, anger, and other emotions, and become stressed themselves, holding these emotions inside. Their little nervous systems get stressed more quickly than our adult systems, and they do not have a way of recognizing or reducing these stresses other than by crying or acting out.

We tell our children to "be tough", essentially telling them to suppress the stress or emotions they are experiencing. This causes their brains to have more trouble processing other events. They then tend to be overly disorganized with their time and their environment. They skip from one task to another, continuously finding other things that need to be done, and forgetting the current task. In children, we see this as constantly moving and getting into everything. In adults we see it as being easily distracted, forgetting to pay bills, missing appointments, always in a hurry but being late anyway. When they get too frustrated and overwhelmed, eventually they can get angry. When we consistently suppress emotions, internal chronic stress levels grow, and various physical symptoms will appear.

Our decision-making and focus center of our brain is in the frontal lobe, or the forehead area. When we are under stress this area is especially affected. A research study at the National Institutes of Mental Health as reported in the New England Journal of Medicine in November 1990, measured brain activity in 25 hyperactive adults. This study found that hyperactive adults had 8% less brain activity in the frontal lobe than normal adults. Hyperactivity was defined as continuous movement with a lack of fine motor coordination. Constant talking, as often seen in hyperactive adults, reflects a lack of inner speech development that can affect social behavior.

Sources of stress in our lives that inhibit learning come from many areas. School or work environments that lack sensory stimulation, lack movement or touch, lack communication opportunities, and lack creative play opportunities, slows the brain communication. Too much competition in sports, creative arts, or test situations affects social ability and self worth. Also TV, computer, and video games stimulate the nervous system but do not have enough physical movement included to reduce the stress they cause. These sources of entertainment also decrease creativity and interactive communication, and increase violence. Other external sources of stress come from a lack of good nutrition, lack of water, and excess electrical fields.

### Stress Depletes Neurotransmitters

When we are stressed our adrenals respond by secreting the hormone adrenalin, causing our muscles to tighten, increasing our heartbeat, preparing us to fight the stress. But in today's society we do not have a way of expelling this adrenalin and it builds up in the tissues causing additional hormonal and neurotransmitter imbalances.

Endorphins are the "feel good" neurotransmitters that are needed to handle stressful situations. When excess stress causes more endorphins to be needed, it creates an imbalance in the level of neurotransmitters. The most common symptoms of this imbalance are increased anxiety or sense of urgency. Then when we feel this added stress, more neurotransmitters are required, furthering the imbalance. Eventually emotional fatigue, most commonly seen as depression sets in.

This is when we begin to get cravings for foods that will help balance the neurotransmitters. One of the most common cravings for food when stressed is chocolate. Chocolate has phenylethylamine, a neurotransmitter that causes feelings of happiness and pleasure. No wonder chocolate is so popular! Research shows that when the brain has adequate supplies of the specific amino acids from certain foods, neurotransmitters stay in balance, helping us to think clearly, focus easier, and sleep well.

Neurotransmitters need to made and used by the nervous system to reduce the effects of stress. ADD symptoms can come from a neurotransmitter imbalance caused by stress or an imbalanced diet. An explanation of the common neurotransmitters, the symptoms related to each one, and some of the foods and nutritional supplements that are used to balance each neurotransmitter is listed. These neurotransmitters are:

## Acetylcholine

Acetylcholine is a neurotransmitter that is needed for improving communication, and maintaining high levels of intelligence, and attention. Acetylcholine regulates your ability to process information. People with good amounts of acetylcholine are highly creative and open to new ideas. They are considerate, are intuitive and innovative, and are quick thinkers. They are very sociable and care highly about their relationships. They are seen as flexible, impulsive, and like to experience new exciting events. They like adventure and they are not afraid of failure.

When there is **too much acetylcholine** people tend to give too much of themselves, and can seem to derive pleasure from being humiliated or mistreated by others or by themselves. They also may tend to become paranoid.

When there is a **deficiency of acetylcholine** memory becomes affected. It becomes more difficult to store information in the brain, and recall names and events when necessary. Some physical issues related to low acetylcholine are Alzheimer's disease, anxiety, autism, speech problems, and reading and writing problems including dyslexia. Dyslexia shows up as reversing letters and numbers, having trouble with math calculations, and reading very slowly with hesitation. Memory issues are a major problem in those with low acetylcholine, including visual and verbal memory. Difficulty concentrating, comprehending, and attention problems also occur, along with mood swings, and impaired judgment when acetylcholine is low.

In adults, some common symptoms of Acetylcholine deficiency are:
- Weakened memory
- Planning activities becomes too difficult
- Avoiding contact with others
- Enhanced tension in relationships that wasn't there before
- Organization, schedules, and daily routines become hard to manage
- You forget names of old friends
- You no longer care about the important people in your life

Besides stress reduction, **specific nutrients can help balance acetylcholine**. They are:
- Alpha Lipoic Acid 100-400mg per day, is an antioxidant that helps to prevent free radicals from affecting the nervous system.
- Acetyl-L-carnitine: 250mg to 1,000mg to raise Acetylcholine levels in the brain.
- CLA, or conjugated linoleic acid, 1,000mg per day helps with metabolism of acetylcholine,

- Phosphatidylcholine: 500mg to 2,000mg/day helps with memory problems.
- Lecithin provides choline with B-complex vitamins to help reduce stress build up in the nervous system.
- Manganese is the mineral that especially helps synthesize acetylcholine.

Foods high in Choline, a B-complex vitamin, which helps create acetylcholine are:

Vegetables: artichokes, broccoli, Brussels sprouts, cabbage, tomatoes

Protein Foods: beef, eggs, shrimp, cod, salmon, pork

Grains: oat bran, wheat bran, wheat germ

Nuts and beans: peanut butter, almonds, macadamia nuts, pine nuts, soy protein powder

## Dopamine

Dopamine is a "feel good" neurotransmitter. Low levels may be experienced as restless boredom. Dopamine determines how well the brain energy works. When it works well the person is a fast thinker, has great reflexes and they are very determined in their actions. They thrive on energy, and are great planners and researchers. They know what they want and tend to be strong-willed. Brainpower is their dominant nature. Games of strategy and thinking suit them well. People with high levels of dopamine may require less sleep than others.

**Low dopamine levels** are found in depression, fatigue, insomnia, high blood pressure, panic attacks, addictions, obesity, diabetes, Parkinson's disease, Alzheimer's, Multiple Sclerosis, Obsessive-Compulsive Disorder, schizophrenia, and Attention Deficit Disorder. The severity of these conditions depends on the level of dopamine deficiency.

Some early physical signs of dopamine deficiency are balance problems, blood sugar instability, junk food cravings, excessive sleep, slow metabolism, and thyroid disorders. With low dopamine the symptoms of anger, guilt, hopelessness, carelessness and aggression show up in the personality, along with depression, mood swings and self-destructive thoughts. Since low dopamine slows processing speed in the brain, there are memory and attention issues related to distractibility, forgetfulness, and failure to be able to follow directions or finish tasks, hyperactivity, impulsive behaviors, decreased alertness, and poor concentration. Even though many of these symptoms are also listed with other neurotransmitter deficiencies, the combination of many of them together signifies a specific dopamine imbalance.

Dopamine is made from the amino acids tyrosine and phenylalanine. These amino acids use the B vitamins folic acid, niacin and vitamin B-6 to make the dopamine bioavailable. **Specific nutrients that increase dopamine levels** in the body are:

- Phenylalanine is the amino acid needed for fatigue, and is best combined with folic acid, iron, B-6, copper, and vitamin C.
- Tyrosine is a dopamine building amino acid and acts as natural pain reliever, increases energy and is supplemented when phenylalanine cannot be absorbed well.
- Rhodiola is an herb that helps rebuild dopamine: 50mg. to 150mg per day
- B-Complex: 25mg to 100mg, with folic acid, niacin (B-3) and B-6, with iron to make dopamine useable.
- CLA (conjugated linoleic acid) omega-6 fatty acid for improved metabolism 2,000mg to 3,000mg/day
- Fish oils, 1,000mg to 3,000mg/day for inflammation

Foods that enhance Phenylalanine and Tyrosine:
    Protein Foods: eggs, turkey, chicken, cottage cheese, pork, whole milk, yogurt (plain non-fat)
    Grains: Granola, oats, wheat germ
    Nuts and beans: dark chocolate

**Norepinephrine** made from adrenalin controls attention and hyperactivity. Stimulating environments and stress increase norepinephrine. Norepinephrine is a "fight or flight" neurotransmitter that increases alertness and the flow of information between brain cells. Hyperactive children do not get enough of this neurotransmitter into the brain because of blood sugar imbalances. Dopamine converts to norepinephrine when Vitamin C is available. So following the nutritional recommendations for dopamine, and adding additional vitamin C foods in the diet, will help to balance norepinephrine.

## GABA (Gamma Amino Butyric Acid).

GABA is a neurotransmitter that helps keep us stable. When in balance the person is a levelheaded, confident, practical, objective team player. They are sensible and take good care of others. They like long term commitments, family traditions, and enjoy their work. When there is a **deficiency of GABA** they physically have digestive changes, chronic pain, protein cravings, decreased libido, and dry mouth. Their personality shows more anxiety, restlessness, obsessive-compulsive disorders, short tempers, poor emotional stability, phobias and fears, and mood swings. They have trouble with verbal memory, concentration, are unable to think clearly, and have short attention spans.

To learn, reason, and remember, our brains need to be able to block out non-important stimuli, and maintain focus. GABA is the neurotransmitter that blocks out unimportant extraneous messages by helping the nervous system focus and respond only to important messages. When you see a movie and you get so absorbed that you forget everything else around you, your GABA neurotransmitters are working.

GABA gives us the control to be fully present, mentally and emotionally, helping to override the adrenalin response. We actually learn to secrete it through practice, so by having quiet focused times regularly, our nervous system can create a habit of GABA secretion. When we do not make the time to slow down and focus on specific tasks, we will become more internally out of balance and become mentally hyperactive. During stressful times when we have too much to do and do not take time to slow down and focus, we become more overwhelmed with life and have trouble thinking. This is where the stress reduction brain exercises in Section Four are very helpful in quickly bringing our body back to focus.

**Supplements that help increase GABA** are 5-HTP, fish oils, vitamin B-6, and the specific GABA amino acids called glutamic acid and glutamine. Foods high in glutamic acid help to improve GABA levels. These foods are:

Fruits and Vegetables: banana, oranges. broccoli, spinach, potato

Protein Foods: beef liver, halibut

Grains: Brown rice, oats, rice bran, whole wheat

Nuts and beans: almonds, lentils, walnuts

## Serotonin

Serotonin is the neurotransmitter that helps to enhance excitement and change in our lives. When we have enough serotonin we like to take on challenges, tend to be physically coordinated, very resourceful, and very realistic. We like to get things done quickly, and like to solve problems. If there is **too much serotonin**, there will be extreme nervousness, distractibility, and feelings of inadequacy especially in relationships. **Deficiency of serotonin** is seen as symptoms of burnout, with abnormal senses. A few of the physical symptoms of serotonin deficiency are difficulty swallowing, hypersensitivity, weight gain, dizziness, drug reactions, and yawning.

Mental and emotional serotonin deficiency shows up as depression, impulsive behavior, lack of common sense, lack of pleasure, codependency, self-absorption and shyness. With serotonin deficiency there is difficulty concentrating, a slow reaction time, restlessness, confusion, memory loss and overwhelm with daily tasks. When you crave carbohydrates you may be low on serotonin, since Serotonin levels are increased by eating carbohydrates.

**Supplements that increase serotonin** levels are:
- 5-HTP: 100mg to 400mg for several weeks
- Calcium: 500mg to 1,000mg with magnesium 200 to 600 mg
- Cod liver oil: 500mg to 2,000mg
- Melatonin: 1/3mg to 6mg
- SAM-e: 50mg to 200mg
- St. John's Wort: 200mg to 600mg

A deficiency in Serotonin affects your other neurotransmitters. You lose your sense of control balanced by dopamine, your memory ability balanced with acetylcholine, and your stability balanced by

GABA. Productive sleep gives you the ability to balance all of the neurotransmitters. Sleep gives the brain the ability to resynchronize every night. It is important to get to sleep early. Our neurotransmitters regenerate between 10 p.m. and 1 a.m., so if we are not sleeping during these hours we will not be able to regenerate healthy levels of neurotransmitters. Sleep disorders are generally caused by serotonin imbalances, but can be related to GABA deficiencies as well.

By matching your symptoms with the corresponding neurotransmitter imbalance you may see a clear picture of a neurotransmitter imbalance. Or it may not be so clear, and other issues may be causing the symptoms. Neurotransmitter deficiencies are very common, yet can change as we change our diet, our habit patterns, or our stressful lifestyles. When you feel out of sorts, and are not sure what direction you are going, this can be a very good indication of a change in your own neurotransmitters. Recognize the recent changes in your life – what foods you are now eating or avoiding, what your current sleep pattern has been, what supplements you are remembering or forgetting to take, and your current stresses or worries. Using this neurotransmitter information can enhance your personal understanding of what causes you to go out of balance.

# Section 2

# *Diet and Nutrition Factors That Improve Learning and Concentration*

# Diet and Nutrition Factors that Improve Learning and Concentration

## Quick Find Outline

# How Does Diet Affect Focus and Thinking Ability?

Many research studies look at the effects of food on behavior. Some of the questions they ask are: Does sugar help improve mental ability or does it cause hyperactivity? Can a lack of focus or concentration come from blood sugar imbalances? How do food additives affect behavior? Are children affected differently than adults? These are all questions we will resolve in this section.

Many times people with Attention Deficit Disorder are more sensitive to foods, especially food additives. They may metabolize carbohydrates differently, depriving the brain of the glucose it needs to think clearly. The brain also needs high quality proteins and essential fats to maintain and grow new brain cell connections.

Yet, the food we eat today contains very little nutrient quality. Not too long ago people farmed and canned their fruits and vegetables so that they could eat them throughout the year. These fruits and vegetables were home grown, or picked ripe from local farmers. When they were canned much of the nutrient quality was still present. Now we buy fruits and vegetables that are grown in other countries, that have been vacuum packed to maintain freshness, or waxed or irradiated so that they do not spoil too quickly. By the time we buy it, and eat it, very little nutrition is left.

Getting good quality nutrition on a regular basis is very important. If we compare how we maintain and care for our cars with how we care for our body, we can make a few interesting correlations. We buy our cars a certain type of gas, and we make sure that there is water in the radiator, and oil in the engine. We know it will not run well, or at all, without these necessities. In fact, our cars have check engine lights that go on when we need to service it. Our body does not have a check engine light, but we can look at our symptoms to know that we need to do something different. Our body needs consistent high quality nutrients, we need water, and we need to keep everything flowing smoothly. Yet, do we do it?

A few years ago the National Cancer Institute began program called **"5 A Day"**, to help us be aware that we need to eat at least 5 servings of fruits and vegetables every day. Most of our antioxidants and minerals come from fruits and vegetables. Stickers showed up on fruits and vegetables, on vegetable bags, and in classrooms around the country. Yet even with this program, an average American is lucky to get 3 to 4 servings per day in their daily diet.

A serving contains one cup of raw, or ½ cup cooked fruits or vegetables. Most bananas are two servings. Many salads contain 2 to 3 cups of vegetables. So it is not impossible to get 5 servings a day. But many people do not eat even an apple a day. One apple contains many nutrients, but it should be fresh. How do you know if it is fresh? Once you begin to eat it, or cut it into pieces, it should begin to turn brown. The browning of the inside of an apple indicates that there are live enzymes in that apple. This is a good indication that it was picked ripe, and still has nutritional benefits.

The many processed convenience foods we eat do not contain the nutrition that we need, and they add chemicals, preservatives, additives, and colorings that are toxic to our liver. Our grains have to be enriched to have vitamins or minerals added back that were lost in the processing. These synthetic or inorganic vitamins and minerals are not metabolized as well those found in real food, so it adds more stress to the digestive system. A paraphrase of an ice cream company's motto used to be, "Do not eat it unless you can pronounce the ingredients in it." The fillers, emulsifiers, gums, and thickening agents are not just unpronounceable, they are a challenge for our digestive system to digest.

Too often we buy enriched cereals hoping that the 100% of our RDA (recommended daily allowance) will be absorbed from that cereal. Since these added vitamins and minerals are inorganic and sprayed on the cereals, very little are actually absorbed by our digestive system. I heard one nutritionist say that in many cases it would probably be more beneficial to eat the box rather than the processed food inside. Hopefully this is not true, but with all of the preservatives and chemicals in our food today, we do have to be aware of what we are buying and eating daily.

### Symptoms of Blood Sugar Imbalance

Blood sugar imbalances such as hypoglycemia can be the cause of brain fog and decreased thinking ability in both children and adults. Eating high carbohydrate foods for breakfast or lunch can cause a quick increase in blood sugar with a corresponding blood sugar drop about 3 hours later. This blood sugar drop is often experienced around 11am, or 3 to 4 pm, or a few hours after eating a high carbohydrate meal. Cereal and milk for breakfast sounds healthy, but if the cereal is low in fiber, and contains a lot of sugar, and the milk is too low in fat, the blood sugar will be affected. A meal of high fiber, whole grains (40%) with protein (30%) and good fat (30%) is the best balance for maintaining a level blood sugar. In one meal I recommend about 5 to 10 grams of fiber. Fiber helps to maintain a steady blood sugar. When too many refined low fiber carbohydrates are eaten, blood sugar rises quickly then falls a few hours later, and this eventually leads to diabetes, but shows up earlier as a lack of mental clarity.

A study in 1995 from the Journal of Pediatric Research looked at glucose levels in a group of children diagnosed with Attention Deficit Disorder and compared them to another group of children. They gave each group a drink containing glucose, the simplest sugar that is absorbed immediately into the bloodstream. Carbohydrates, even complex carbohydrates like whole wheat and starchy vegetables, are eventually broken down into glucose. In this study both groups of children produced a sharp increase in blood sugar, which then caused a sharp increase in blood insulin levels, and a consequent drop in blood sugar levels.

When insulin levels go down, the neurotransmitter norepinephrine is supposed to be secreted to help get more blood glucose to the brain to compensate for the drop in blood sugar. It was found that in the children diagnosed with Attention Deficit Disorder, the expected rise in norepinephrine was only 50%. As we read in the previous section, norepinephrine is a "fight or flight" neurotransmitter that improves alertness and circulation of information between brain cells. The children with ADD were not getting enough of this neurotransmitter into their brain because of their reaction to blood sugar. Also we learned in the last section that norepinephrine helps to balance dopamine, the major neurotransmitter associated with ADD. So blood sugar imbalances can cause lowered blood glucose in the brain affecting thinking, focusing, and decision-making ability

We are going to look at all the effects of blood sugar imbalances so that you will be able to tell if your blood sugar is causing some of your ADD symptoms. A fasting blood test will show if you are prone to diabetes or insulin resistance (pre-diabetes). Now type II diabetes is diagnosed when blood sugar levels are consistently over 125. If your fasting blood sugar is between 100 and 125 then you fall into the pre-diabetic range. Fasting blood sugar readings taken before eating in the morning should be under 100. **Hypoglycemic reactions** occur when your blood sugar drops after a high carbohydrate meal, and your blood sugar level goes down under 60. This is low blood sugar where you have symptoms of faintness, perspiration, lightheadness, and clammy skin.

If you do not have diabetes or borderline fasting blood glucose levels over 100, how do you know if you have blood sugar problems? Here is a general list of **common symptoms of blood sugar imbalances**:
- Mental confusion with problems thinking clearly
- Heart palpitations and/or rapid heartbeat
- Headaches
- Anxiety and/or depression
- Nausea
- Unexplained sweating
- Hunger and food cravings
- Mood swings and/or irritability
- Increased thirst
- Vision problems

- Impaired coordination
- Chronic fatigue

If you have a number of these symptoms, monitor your blood sugar, and learn to use the Glycemic Load Chart to improve your diet for at least one month and see if it makes a difference. Preventing blood sugar problems with diet is very effective and can stop the progression that leads to diabetes.

Blood sugar and insulin balance affect our mental and emotional energy balances. **Insulin resistance**, also called pre-diabetes, happens over time as people lose their sensitivity to insulin, which is largely due to the excessive amount of sugar and refined carbohydrates found in the typical American diet. Are your cells sensitive to insulin? When they are not sensitive, the insulin levels stay in balance. But, when your cells are sensitive to insulin and you eat carbohydrates, your liver will take up as much sugar as it can hold, and excess sugar will be turned into triglycerides and cholesterol. This is one of the major causes of high cholesterol and triglycerides.

When you eat too many carbohydrates in a meal you may get symptoms of insulin fluctuations. The excess sugar causes insulin to increase rapidly. This excess insulin moves sugar into the cells too quickly leaving less in your bloodstream, and when your blood sugar drops you become hypoglycemic. When your insulin levels fluctuate too often you may get one or more of the following hypoglycemic symptoms: insomnia, foggy thinking, irritability, perspiring skin, heart palpitations, lightheadedness, panic attacks, and sugar cravings.

If you continue to eat many imbalanced meals containing too much sugar, refined carbohydrates, and processed foods, your insulin levels remain higher than normal between meals. This happens because the excess sugar and fats, stored in your cells, make your cells believe they have stored-up energy available that is not being used. When there is too much stored energy, your blood sugar will not fluctuate and your insulin levels will remain higher causing partial insulin resistance. Now the food you eat will be stored as fat instead of being used as energy. Common symptoms of insulin levels staying high are: depression, decreased memory, irritability, water retention, weight gain, and fluctuating blood pressure readings.

When you have sustained high levels of insulin then you are insulin resistant. At this point your cells are overly filled with fats and sugar and they barely respond to insulin. Symptoms of insulin resistance are persistent high blood pressure, abnormal cholesterol readings including high triglycerides and low HDL, type II diabetes, excess weight in the abdominal area, and plague build-up in your coronary arteries and brain. You will also have trouble thinking clearly, since your brain is not able to absorb glucose that it needs to function well.

At this point your pancreas will slow down its production of insulin, causing the blood sugar level to stay up, resulting in type II diabetes. So a diet high in carbohydrates and low in fat can lead to chronic hypoglycemia, which eventually causes an insulin imbalance, ultimately leading to diabetes, in which the pancreas cannot use insulin effectively. An estimated 25% of the population is believed to be insulin resistant to some degree, and some researchers believe the number may be as high as 75%.

Insulin balance is important for other functions too. Insulin builds muscle and stores protein. Insulin also stores magnesium. Magnesium is important in maintaining a healthy blood pressure. But when your cells become resistant to insulin, you cannot store it and it is lost through urination. Magnesium is also important in creating cellular energy that helps to manufacture insulin. So even when you take excess magnesium it may not get into the cells if they are too insulin resistant.

It is important to get a balanced diet of complex carbohydrates, high quality protein, and good fats on a daily basis. When certain carbohydrate foods digest, they turn to sugar in the bloodstream very quickly. This is what causes a quick rise in blood sugar, and then insulin is needed to metabolize that blood sugar into the cells for energy. Yet high insulin levels will rob the brain of sugar also. Cravings for sugar increase when we need to focus our brain activity. When sugars cannot be used by the brain then fatigue, a lack of focus, and poor concentration are common symptoms. Insulin imbalances also affect serotonin levels that regulate moods.

## Glycemic Load Food List

The glycemic load number is used to measure the actual level of blood sugar raising power per serving of food. The glycemic load value of each food is calculated by multiplying the glycemic index value by the average grams of carbohydrates per serving, and dividing the total by 100. One glycemic load unit equals approximately one gram of glucose. Add up your glycemic load points each day to see if you are eating more than the average of 60 to 100 units per day. Over 150 glycemic load units regularly per day will eventually cause blood sugar imbalances. Ideally, it is recommended to consume about 50 to no more than 80 grams of glycemic load units per day to help balance current blood sugar problems.

Unprocessed, nonstarchy vegetables have a naturally low glycemic load number. The more processed a vegetable is, for example when it is juiced, the higher the glycemic number. Also more starchy vegetables have a higher glycemic load number since they contain more carbohydrates. Many vegetables are not included in this list because they have so little carbohydrates that their glycemic load number are zero. Some of these low glycemic vegetables include romaine lettuce, kale, onion, and avocados.

As you can see from the list, meats, eggs, and other mainly protein foods are not listed on the Glycemic Load Chart. These foods do not increase your blood sugar reading. Also fats, such as butter and vegetable oils, also are not individually listed since they do not increase blood sugar.

Processed cereals have on average a high glycemic load value. Cereals have a lot of carbohydrates, and so the best ones are the higher fiber cereals, or the less processed whole grain cereals. Whole oats, versus instant oatmeal, will have a lower glycemic load number. Dried fruits in cereals will increase the glycemic load number because of the concentrated sugar they contain.

Most dairy products are well balanced between carbohydrates and proteins and fats. So the glycemic load value of ice cream is less than many other snack foods. Adding dairy products to processed cereals will help to balance the glycemic value for that meal, yet the total glycemic load points would be around 30 points for just that one meal. And that is with just one serving of cereal and milk. Many people eat more than the recommended serving amounts for processed cereals.

The Glycemic Load Chart contains a long list of snack foods. This is to show that some of the low fat snack foods, like pretzels and rice cakes, have higher glycemic numbers, and some of the higher fat foods like peanuts and cashews, have lower glycemic numbers. Then of course, there are some high fat snack foods like potato and corn chips that have many carbohydrates and high glycemic load numbers.

The beverage category on the Glycemic Load chart includes juices, soft drinks, and smoothies. The drinks with sugar added have higher glycemic numbers. Any time sugar in any form is added to drinks or foods the glycemic load numbers will be higher.

The Glycemic Load chart on the next page is designed to help you make better decisions on daily food choices. The foods that are rated at 10 or less are the low glycemic load foods. These are the best food choices. The medium range foods with a glycemic load number between 11 and 19 are to be used cautiously. Any food on the list with over 20 glycemic load points per serving is very high in blood sugar raising power. These are the foods to avoid. Ideally, you should try to keep your glycemic load points between 50 and 80 daily to keep your insulin and blood sugar in balance. A consistent low glycemic load diet will give you more sustained energy throughout the day.

## Glycemic Load Chart

|  | Glycemic Load per serving |
|---|---|
| High glycemic load (worse foods) | 20 |
| Medium glycemic load | 11 to 19 |
| Low glycemic load (best foods) | 10 or less |

Fruits

| | |
|---|---|
| Apple, 1 average | 6 |
| Apricots, dried | 8 |
| Banana, 1 whole | 12 |
| Cantaloupe | 4 |
| Cherries, 1 cup | 3 |
| Fruit cocktail, canned | 9 |
| Grapefruit, fresh | 3 |
| Grapefruit juice, unsweetened | 9 |
| Grapes, 1 cup | 8 |
| Kiwi, fresh | 6 |
| Orange | 5 |
| Orange Juice, 8 oz. | 12 |
| Peach | 5 |
| Pear | 4 |
| Pineapple | 7 |
| Prunes, pitted | 10 |
| Raisins, 1/2 cup | 28 |
| Strawberries, 1 cup | 1 |
| Strawberry Jam, 1 T | 10 |
| Strawberry Fruit Bars | 23 |
| Watermelon | 4 |

Vegetables

| | |
|---|---|
| Asparagus (6 spears) | 1 |
| Broccoli, 1/2 cup steamed | 1 |
| Cabbage, 1 cup raw | 1 |
| Carrots, 1 cup raw | 3 |

| | |
|---|---|
| Carrot juice, 8 oz. | 10 |
| Corn on the cob, 1 ear | 9 |
| French Fries, 1/2 cup | 22 |
| Green Beans, 1/2 cup boiled | 1 |
| Green Peas, 1/2 cup boiled | 3 |
| Potato, baked, white | 26 |
| Spinach, 1/2 cup steamed | 1 |
| Sweet Potato | 17 |
| Tomatoes, 1 cup raw | 1 |

Beans

| | |
|---|---|
| Baked Beans | 16 |
| Garbanzo Beans | 10 |
| Kidney Beans | 7 |
| Navy Beans | 12 |
| Soy Beans | 1 |

Grains

| | |
|---|---|
| Bagel, white, 2 oz. | 23 |
| Blueberry Muffin | 17 |
| Corn muffin | 30 |
| Corn tortilla | 12 |
| Croissant | 17 |
| Doughnut, cake type | 17 |
| Egg noodles | 18 |
| English muffin | 11 |
| Hamburger bun | 9 |
| Macaroni and Cheese | 32 |
| Pumpernickel bread, 1 slice | 8 |
| Rice, brown, 1 cup cooked | 18 |
| Rice, white, 1 cup cooked | 23 |
| Spaghetti, boiled, 1 cup | 18 |
| Taco shell, cornmeal based | 8 |
| Waffles, one 7" round | 21 |
| White bread, 1 slice | 10 |
| Whole Grain bread, 1 slice | 7 |

Cereals

| | |
|---|---|
| All-Bran, 1 cup | 9 |
| Cheerios, 1 cup | 15 |
| Coco- Pops, 1 cup | 36 |
| Corn Pops, 1 cup | 21 |
| Corn Flakes, 1 cup | 27 |
| Cream of Wheat, 1 cup | 22 |
| Fruit Loops, 1 cup | 18 |
| Grape Nuts, 1 cup | 16 |
| Life, 1 Cup | 16 |
| Oat Bran, 1 cup | 3 |
| Oatmeal, 1 cup | 16 |
| Raisin Bran, 1 cup | 27 |
| Rice Krispies, 1 cup | 21 |
| Shredded Wheat, 1 cup | 15 |
| Special K, 1 cup | 14 |
| Sustain Cereal Bar, 1 cup | 14 |
| Total, 1 cup | 17 |

Snack Foods

| | |
|---|---|
| Angel Food Cake, 1 slice | 19 |
| Cashews, salted, 2 oz. | 3 |
| Chocolate Cake with frosting | 20 |
| Corn chips | 17 |
| Fruit Roll-ups | 24 |
| Graham crackers | 14 |
| Jelly Beans | 22 |
| M&M Peanuts | 6 |
| Peanuts, 2 oz. | 1 |
| Popcorn, microwaved plain | 4 |
| Pop Tarts, Chocolate | 25 |
| Potato chips | 11 |
| Pound cake, 1 slice | 15 |
| Power Bar | 24 |
| Pretzels | 16 |

| | |
|---|---|
| Rice cakes | 17 |
| Rye Crisp cracker | 11 |
| Skittles | 32 |
| Snickers Bar | 23 |
| Soda crackers | 12 |
| Vanilla wafers | 14 |
| Wheat Thins | 12 |

Dairy Products

| | |
|---|---|
| Ensure, Vanilla, 8 oz. | 12 |
| Ice Cream, 1 cup | 8 |
| Milk, 2%, 1cup | 4 |
| Reduced fat yogurt with fruit | 10 |
| Soy milk, 8 oz. | 8 |

Beverages

| | |
|---|---|
| Apple Juice, 8 oz. | 12 |
| Orange Juice, 8 oz. | 13 |
| Gatorade, 8 oz. | 12 |
| Pepsi, 8 oz. | 15 |
| Smoothie, Strawberry | 14 |
| Tomato juice, 1/2 cup | 4 |

Use the glycemic load chart to choose your foods wisely. Remember, this chart contains common foods that will either help maintain a stable blood sugar or cause it to go out of balance. The fiber content is a factor in determining the glycemic load number. Whole fruits and vegetables, and whole grains, have lower numbers since they contain the most fiber, thereby raising blood sugar more slowly.

Strive to get as much fiber as possible from fresh vegetables and small amounts of whole grains. Refined grain and processed food consumption should be minimal. Meals should be small and frequent in order to keep blood sugar at a normal level. Protein should be included with each meal and snack so that blood sugar is maintained throughout the day. Most of our trouble stabilizing blood sugar comes from the added sugars in processed foods. Now we will look at the overall effects of different types of sugar contained in many of our natural and processed foods.

# What Are the Effects of Sugar?

As a parent, I know from personal experience, that excessive sugary foods affect children's behavior. Sugary foods served at holidays such as Halloween, Valentine's Day, Christmas, and Easter can create behavior changes that can make the holiday season seem more stressed than it should be. Recent studies show that 30% of our foods are basically high sugar, high carbohydrate junk foods, and children are some of the worst offenders. Yale University School of Medicine is studying the effect of sugar on children, and is seeing an increase in the release of adrenaline from the adrenals, creating symptoms of anxiety, concentration problems, shakiness, and restlessness. Also increased brain wave fluctuations measured after high sugar consumption indicates a decline in the ability to focus.

**Sugars** and other sweeteners are used in most processed foods today. Sugar can be hidden as many different names such as sucrose, fructose, maltodextrin, maltose, lactose, and high fructose corn syrup. All of these are names of refined sugars. If a food you are buying has any of these names on the label as the first ingredient, or a combination of them as one of the first four ingredients, do not buy it! It will cause blood sugar imbalances over time, and affect your immune system.

Refined sugars are added to many foods to improve the taste. Sugar consumption has increase dramatically since the 1950's. The U.S. Department of Agriculture estimated in 1993 that the average American ate 130 pounds of sugar per year, in 1998 it went to 147 pounds of sugar, and now this number is around 170 pounds of sugar per year. This includes whole sugar and forms of processed sugars.

Our body, especially our brain, uses **glucose** for energy. Glucose is found in fruits and vegetables, and is used in the metabolism of all plants and animals. Many of the carbohydrate foods listed on the Glycemic Load Chart are converted into glucose in our body. Glucose that is circulating through our bloodstream is called blood sugar. Other forms of sugars are found in different types of foods. Sugar made from corn and other starchy vegetables is called dextrose. In whole fruits we find fructose as the major sugar component. Maltose comes from malt sugar. Lactose is found naturally in milk sugar. Sucrose is the refined sugar made from sugar cane and sugar beets.

When starches and complex sugars from whole food sources are digested, they are broken down into simple sugars called monosaccharides, which are beneficial sugars. Yet when refined starches and sugars are eaten together they break down through fermentation, creating carbon dioxide, acetic acid, alcohol and water in our digestive tract. This often is the cause of indigestion problems.

**High fructose corn syrup** was developed in 1966 as a sweetener to blend into processed foods. It is made from cornstarch and turns into fructose and glucose. Yet fructose is metabolized differently than glucose and the over-consumption of fructose can contribute to high triglycerides and insulin resistance. Fructose found in whole fruits does not have the adverse affect of processed fructose, and should not contribute to higher blood fats. But we are getting processed fructose more often as an additive in foods. The consumption of high fructose corn syrup increased to an average of 62.6 pounds per person in 2001.

Many people actually use sugar as medicine. Sugar tends to change the way our metabolism uses specific amino acids to make neurotransmitters. Eating refined carbohydrates increase the level of the amino acid tryptophan, which helps to create the neurotransmitter serotonin. Serotonin is the calming neurotransmitter. So when we need to relax we will crave sugar so that we can create more serotonin. This is one of the main reasons sugar is so addictive.

Excess sugar affects every organ in the body, especially the liver. First the liver stores sugar, or glucose, for energy. If too much is consumed then the liver will physically enlarge to store the excess. When it is filled to its maximum capacity the liver will store the glycogen as fatty acids. These fatty acids show up as excess triglycerides and/or cholesterol, and are stored in specific areas of the body. Excess triglycerides can be seen as extra inches around the abdomen due to fat storage by the liver. Cholesterol builds up in the arteries as it protects the body from these dangerous fatty acids. There are essential fatty acids that can help to reduce these dangerous fatty acids, but reducing sugar intake is the first step in really removing them.

Eventually these dangerous fatty acids affect the circulatory system including the functioning of the heart and kidneys. As circulation is impaired, a variety of problems can occur. Stiffness, back pain, shortness of breath, memory loss, immune weakness, and abnormal blood pressure are common complaints. Too much sugar does affect our brain function. B-complex vitamins are needed to process glutamic acid, which is needed by the brain, and they are also cancelled out by excessive sugar. If you get sleepy after eating, or cannot think clearly, look at the level of refined foods in your meals to see what may be causing it to occur.

Eating sugar is worse than eating nothing. Do not eat sugar-based foods just to try to get food into your system. Soft drinks are one of the worst drinks to consume on a regular basis. The average can of soda pop contains eight to nine teaspoons of sugar. This amount of sugar that is usually consumed in a very short period of time creates havoc with sugar metabolism in the liver. In response, the body must mobilize large amounts of adrenalin and insulin to clear the sugar from the bloodstream. Fruit juices are not much better. Juices contain about the same amount of sugar as soft drinks. They are basically sugar water with very few nutrients. Drinking juices or soft drinks regularly can lead to significant health problems as well as blood sugar disorders.

I remember one office visit I had with a mother and two sons early in the morning. The mother brought her sons in to be tested for hyperactivity symptoms. Both boys were between 8 and 12 years old and could not sit still. They were fidgeting with their hands and could not sit quietly even during the testing procedure. Finally when I could not test one of them using Electro-Dermal Screening, I asked the mother what these boys had eaten for breakfast that day. Each of them had eaten a candy bar and a bottle of Coca-cola. That is when we stopped testing and had a long conversation about nutrition. When we eat the amount of sugar in a candy bar and a soft drink such as a Coca-cola, it lowers the immune system function for 6 hours. These two boys were going to school with a weakened immune system, and a stressed nervous system. It was not a surprise that they were having trouble sitting still and learning. I advised the mother to change the boys breakfast, or it would not do any good to give them a homeopathic remedy for their hyperactivity. Their diet had to be improved first.

When too much sugar is mixed with protein-based foods other reactions occur. When pure proteins are digested, they are broken down into amino acids, which are needed to rebuild cells daily. Yet when proteins are taken with excess refined sugar, they become rancid, creating other chemical poisons our body has to detoxify. Our liver spends much of its time breaking down these chemical poisons, creating common symptoms of bad breath, bloating, an accumulation of gas in the intestines, and foul smelling perspiration.

If you are tired all the time, look at your level of sugar consumption and foods that turn to sugar quickly in your system. I know sugar based foods can lift your energy quickly, but over time they will cause adrenal stress, hypoglycemia, and eventually diabetes, heart disease, and chronic fatigue. We have already looked at how important it is to keep your blood sugar in balance to maintain a consistent energy level. As listed on the Glycemic Load Chart, other carbohydrates, especially processed carbohydrates turn into glucose in the digestive system and can cause the same fatigue as eating pure sugar.

Sugar added to foods makes the food more acidic, which creates the formation of excess acids in our cells. When too many acids are produced it interferes with the production of oxygen into our cells creating blood sugar problems, concentration problems, and immune and nervous system disorders. Sugar based foods also cause excess free radical formation that increases cell damage, and lowers our digestive enzymes activity, specifically affecting protein absorption. This can cause muscle weakness and pain.

When sugar is added to natural foods it deprives them of their own nutrients. Sugar is more than empty calories, it is hazardous to our health because it uses up the natural nutrients normally found in our foods. More minerals, antioxidants and B-complex vitamins are needed in higher amounts when sugar is in the diet. Sugar can upset the body's mineral balance, especially of chromium, calcium and magnesium. This is one reason I do not like any type of processed sugars to be used in chewable or liquid, vitamin or mineral formulas. The sugar or fructose added to improve the taste reduces the actual amount of nutrients in the supplement.

The major minerals, calcium, magnesium, sodium and potassium, are needed to maintain the normal acid / alkaline levels. When we are acid from eating too many sugar based foods, calcium will be borrowed from our teeth and bones to maintain a balanced pH level. Over time this will cause bone deterioration and tooth decay. Magnesium is needed to metabolize calcium, and is needed by our muscles to function, and so will be used up causing muscle aches and pains when we are too acid.

Children with "growing pains" felt in their legs may want to look at sugar levels in their diet. A lack of minerals often causes these pains in the Achilles tendon area of the calf muscle. Potassium and sodium imbalances in our cellular fluids will also cause headaches, fluid retention and joint stiffness. This is one reason that headaches are a common complaint during sugar withdrawal. The sodium and potassium levels are shifting and until they come back into balance there will be a tendency toward headaches.

One Saturday morning, I saw a 1st grader who was complaining of pains in his legs around the Achilles tendons. "Elvis" (not his real name) and I talked about what he was eating. He said he had some sugar cereal that morning and he was "hyper" from it. He realizes, even as 1st grader, the effects of sugar on his behavior. When I told him that he may be having growing pains, and that sugar was not going to help him grow taller, he said he better stay away from the sugary cereal.

Overuse of sugar in adults and children causes the adrenals to work harder, putting out more adrenaline than is necessary. With excess adrenaline there is a feeling of constant stress and anxiety in adults. In children it is seen as hyperactivity, concentration difficulties, and irritability. Concentration is affected because brain wave activity increases and focusing on one subject becomes more difficult. Over time, when the brain cells have been stressed too long, symptoms of depression will begin to occur. At this stage the whole system becomes overwhelmed, causing symptoms of fatigue and indifference, signaling that we need a rest. If depression is caused by excess refined sugar intake, no matter what medication is taken, the symptoms will not be alleviated properly.

# What about Food Additives and Preservatives?

Keeping blood sugar in balance is important, yet looking the availability of nutrients contained in the foods we eat is also important. Too many processed foods are enriched, adding inorganic minerals and vitamins to compensate for the nutrition lost in the processing of the food. Some people believe enriched foods are good enough, and we will be able to absorb their nutrients sufficiently to benefit from them. But what about the great increase in type II diabetes in the past few years, seen especially now in children? What about the increase in Attention Deficit Disorder and behavioral problems in schools? Adults are now getting symptoms of Alzheimer's more quickly than before, and are suffering from chronic diseases earlier in life.

Many of these issues are caused by lack of bioavailable nutrition in our diet. Our digestive system tries to absorb nutrients from the foods we eat. Depending on the state of the food – baked, broiled, microwaved, or the additives added, our body can actually get more stressed eating foods that are hard for our liver to metabolize. This is why the National Cancer Institute keeps raising the number of fruits and vegetables recommended daily to prevent cancer, and keep our immune system healthy. This is another reason we are seeing earlier signs of indigestion and heartburn in children. The foods we put in our body have so many preservatives, and chemicals, and not enough real nutrition to be beneficial.

People with Attention Deficit Disorder need concentrated whole food nutrition. They need to get real foods, not processed foods, in their diet. The first suggestion I tell parents who are struggling with a hyperactive child is to stay away from any food colorings, especially the added colorings in juices, cereals, snacks, and vitamin supplements. These food colorings affect the functioning of the nervous system. Our liver cannot break down these chemicals and they affect our neurotransmitters, and eventually our thinking ability. It is amazing the amount of food coloring found in processed foods. For example, new green ketchup was recently added to our condiment choices. I do not believe it lasted on the market very long, because we could not get used to green ketchup. But to make the ketchup green they had to add 150mg. of green food coloring to each tablespoon of ketchup. One study done on the effects of food coloring published in the Archives of Disease in Childhood in June of 2004, used just 20 mg of food coloring per day to determine if hyperactivity increased in three year old children. They found significant increases in hyperactivity at only 20 mg. of food coloring per day, so I cannot imagine what the green ketchup did to the children who used it.

When **food additives** are added to natural foods both physical and behavioral problems can occur. The three most common symptoms found when we get too many food additives are headaches, anxiety, and upset stomach. Common food additives to watch out for, beside food colorings, are preservatives, artificial sweeteners, and caffeine. **Preservatives** are found in all processed foods, and even in some of the natural foods such as fruits and vegetables. It is difficult to get all fresh food unless you grow it yourself. Preservatives prevent spoilage of food so that it can be transported from the farm or factory to our grocery stores. Preservatives are either anti-microbial or antioxidants. Antimicrobial preservatives prevent the growth of molds, yeasts and bacteria on the food. Antioxidants keep foods from becoming rancid, turning brown, or developing black spots.

Consumers often question the safety of preservatives, and so the FDA has to keep lists of the different preservatives and food additives. They look at the potential levels of toxicity of the preservative, the amount of preservatives needed for each food, and if there is a danger of getting too much of one food additive from eating the same types of foods.

Sodium nitrite is a preservative used as an anti-microbial in meats. It is combined with salt to prevent botulism. Sodium nitrite also gives processed meats their color. Otherwise hot dogs and ham would be a gray-green color, and they would not look appetizing.

BHA and BHT are preservatives used as antioxidants. They slow down the decay of flavor, odor, and color changes caused by oxidation. They are used mostly in foods that have natural oils, and in dry cereals. Sulfites are another type of antioxidant preservative that is used to prevent or slow down the discoloration of fruits and vegetables, and are often used at salad bars. People who are sensitive to sulfites usually get an asthma attack reaction when they eat foods with sulfites.

Other food additives help to improve the taste or texture of foods, or maintain the stability of a food. Acid regulators like acetic acid help keep the flavor and stop the growth of bacteria on the food. Xanthan gum is one of the thickeners commonly used. Coloring agents can be organic such as beets (red), lycopenes (red), or tumeric (yellow); or inorganic red, blue, and yellow dyes can be used. Emulsifiers, like polysorbate 80, keep foods from separating into oil and water. Propylene glycol is a humectant that keeps moisture in the foods to prevent them from drying out. Polyethylene glycol is an antifoaming agent used to maintain the density of the food. MSG is a flavoring agent to improve the taste, as are sweeteners such as maltodextrin and dextrose.

The FDA generally regards each of these food additives as safe, at least in small quantities. But when combining them in foods and then looking at the potential cumulative effect, we have to realize that the more preservative and food additives we get on a daily basis, the more our liver has to detoxify. That is why headaches and bloating are common symptoms of too many food additives.

Each of these food additives has to be processed through our liver. Our liver has the task to remove toxins from our tissues including our digestive system. Then it has to make the toxins water soluble to get them ready to be released through the kidneys or colon. When the liver is overloaded, or is not supported with enough dietary antioxidants, it cannot detoxify our tissues and it can actually grow larger and become clogged. Certain fruits and vegetables help the liver complete detoxification. This is why we need to have regular amounts of fruits and vegetables daily. The bioflavonoids found in fruits and vegetables help to move the toxins out of the tissues, and cruciferous vegetables such as broccoli, cauliflower, kale, and Brussels sprouts help to make them water soluble to get them out of the body. We need a variety of fruits and vegetables daily to get rid of food additives and preservatives.

Processed foods also have many fillers, such as modified food starch or guar gum that are hard to digest. Our digestive system has to find a way to process these fillers, and when it has trouble it will often create symptoms of bloating, abdominal pains, diarrhea or constipation, and allergies. Over time some people get so sensitive to foods that they feel like they are allergic to everything. They get nauseated eating most foods and so have to limit what they can consume, often missing out on many nutrients.

Our small intestine is in charge of taking the food that is processed in the stomach, pulling out the nutrients, and removing the waste to the large intestine. When the food cannot be processed well in the stomach, it causes inflammation in the small intestine. This is what causes excess gas and bloating after eating certain foods. Our small intestine gets inflamed with too much processed food, and reacts by creating a mucus layer over the wall of the intestine to prevent damage from the inflammation. Eventually this mucus layer builds up, and creates diarrhea, and sensitivities to many foods since they are not digested well. This is why it is so important to eat foods that do not have many fillers or preservatives. Each of these starches, chemicals, and food dyes stress the small intestine, and cause food sensitivity reactions.

**Allergic reactions to foods** can also cause behavioral symptoms of Attention Deficit Disorder. The most common foods people become sensitive to are milk, eggs, wheat, peanuts, and soy products. We get sensitive to these foods due to the way they are processed. Wheat products are found in many foods, not just breads. Wheat is used as a thickening agent as wheat gluten in soups and cereals. Most of the time wheat has been processed so much that it loses its nutrient quality and has to be "enriched." Milk is so altered during pasteurization that we lose the enzymes needed to digest the proteins well, which causes mucus to build up in the lymph tissues, often showing up as chronic sinus drainage, abdominal pain, bloating, and diarrhea. Soybeans are being used in many processed foods as fillers, and are now found in many low carbohydrate foods as soy protein. Too much soy can affect the thyroid and metabolism of nutrients, especially minerals.

When I do testing on children for food sensitivities I like to test the actual foods that they are eating. I use Kinesiology (muscle testing) on younger clients, and Electro Dermal Screening on older clients. I can use testing vials to measure sensitivities to many pure foods like apples, wheat, and peanuts. But most of us do not eat pure foods. Our apples are in applesauce, our wheat is processed in bread, and our peanuts are found in peanut butter. So clients bring in the actual foods that they eat, and we find out which ones are truly beneficial, which means that they reduce their stress level. Other foods that are tested will not make a change one way or another on their stress level. These foods are okay to eat. The sensitive or "allergic" foods are the ones that create more stress to the system. These foods create a reaction during testing that corresponds to an increased stress response.

When the foods that stress the body are eliminated many adults and children find that their energy level and mood improve greatly. I remember one young boy; I will call "Bobby", I tested on a Friday afternoon. His mother brought in all the foods that he would eat. We eliminated some of his favorites, but not all of them. By Monday morning he was already acting differently, and his teacher wanted to know what medication he was on. But he wasn't taking anything. He had just taken out of his diet the few foods that were causing him to be hyperactive.

Among the many factors that shape the lives of children, nutrition often plays a critical role. What children eat during their growing years has a great effect on the way they think, learn, and act. Many studies have found, for example, that children with higher intakes of antioxidants, B vitamins and minerals do better in school than those children whose diets are lower in these nutrients. Others studies show that children who are exposed to too many environmental chemicals or heavy metals in the air and water have more trouble learning and remembering, and have more nervous system disorders.

The **Feingold program** is a children's nutritional program that recommends a diet based on foods that do not contain artificial flavors, preservatives, and food colorings. Numerous research studies found that symptoms of Attention Deficit Hyperactivity Disorder improved between 50 and 70% of the time while children followed this nutritional program.

One study, published in Lancet in 1985, showed that 79% of hyperactive children had symptoms improve when food chemicals were removed from their diet. Then when the food chemicals were re-introduced the symptoms returned. Sugar was found to have a similar detrimental effect as food chemicals. In controlled studies done at juvenile correctional facilities in the 1980s, they found that behavior improved in 47% of the 12 facilities that took part in the Feingold program, which included over 8000 juveniles.

Other similar studies show that when students are put on a healthy diet, with nutrient dense foods like whole grains, vegetables, and fruits, and avoid sugar and artificial colors, flavors, and preservatives, the improvement in their behavior is tremendous and their academic scores can improve. One of the largest studies was done with students during the early 1980's in New York City public schools. All of the children in over 800 public schools gradually eliminated all artificial colors and flavors, certain preservatives such as BHT and BHA, and reduced the amount of sugar available in school lunches. Their scores on standardized achievement tests improved from 39th percentile to the 55th percentile in four years. This improvement was also seen in grade level performance in the normal classroom setting. And all of this was done without changing their diet at home. So even a small improvement in getting whole food nutrition in the body can improve learning.

# *Balancing the Daily Diet*

Our brain has 200 billion cells that need specific nutritional requirements for daily operation. We need proteins for amino acids, and carbohydrates for glucose, and a number of different vitamins and minerals, and water. Good fats are also important for brain function, especially to make cholesterol needed by our brain more than any other part of the body. Any dietary shortage of necessary nutrients can have a great impact on brain function.

During pregnancy it is vitally important for the mother to be sure to get high quality nutrients, or the child has a greater chance to be born with some brain and nervous system imbalances. Some symptoms seen in young children, such as slow learning, aggressiveness, or hyperactivity can be brought on by a lack of good quality nutrition in the mother during pregnancy. Folic acid is a B-vitamin that now is highly recommended during pregnancy to prevent birth defects. Yet, a full complement of the B-vitamins along with antioxidants and minerals are what is really needed by every pregnant mother.

As the baby grows into a toddler, nutrition continues to be very important also. The brain develops primarily during the first five years of life, and lack of nutrition during these years can have an impact on the ability to learn when the child reaches school age.

Because of differences in the way our body processes food, most of us are quite deficient in certain nutrients and overloaded in others. Even with an ideal diet, most of us have certain nutrients that are at very low levels, and may need much more than the RDA to achieve a healthy level. The nutrients in overload must be carefully avoided in vitamin supplements or serious health problems can develop. Due to stress factors, genetic patterns, and metabolism, these deficiencies or excesses are different for many people. This is why one drug or nutrient does not work for everyone. Understanding different metabolic factors helps to put into perspective the needs of each person. Some of the common nutrients that can be too high in some people, and low in others are calcium, iron, folic acid, copper, manganese, choline, methionine, and omega-6 fatty acids.

Some metabolic factors that affect neurotransmitters and create different symptoms of Attention Deficit Disorder are over-methylation, under-methylation, and malabsorption. **Methylation** is a biochemical process that involves modifying a DNA molecule by adding a methyl group. Methylation is like a spark plug on a car. If the spark plug does not activate, the engine will not run. Methylation uses metabolic chemicals and amino acids to create internal reactions that are necessary for our body to function well.

When these spark plug-like reactions are increased there is **over-methylation**, which causes symptoms of anxiety with depression. Over-methylation also creates excessive levels of the neurotransmitters dopamine, norepinephrine and serotonin. Other symptoms of over-methylation are lack of motivation and drive, food and chemical sensitivities, upper body pain, and adverse reactions to anti-depressive drugs and supplements such as Prozac, Paxil, Zoloft, St. John's Wort, and SAMe. These people do better with more folic acid, niacin, and vitamin B-12.

When there are not enough methyl reactions, often caused by excess free radicals and oxidative stress, we get **under-methylated**. This is associated with low serotonin levels. These people can tend to be obsessive-compulsive, be more rebellious, or disobedient, and suffer from seasonal allergies and depression. They will want to be a perfectionist and be more competitive, but will not have the energy to do it, and will get frustrated. These people will also suffer from more chronic illnesses such as heart disease, cancer, and premature aging. They benefit from calcium, magnesium, vitamin B-6, and methionine, an amino acid used in methylation. SAM-e, St. John's Wort, or Kava Kava, are supplements that help improve methylation levels.

It is best to keep methylation in a balanced state by reducing stress levels, and getting enough antioxidants to reduce excess free radicals. S-adenosyl-L-methionine (SAMe) is created in our body by combining ATP energy and the amino acid methionine. If methylation is out of balance, the homocysteine level will increase, causing heart and circulatory problems, but also a greater tendency to Alzheimer's disease.

**Malabsorption** is another metabolic factor that can create Attention Deficit problems. There are three ways our digestive system can have a problem with absorbing foods. In the stomach, we can have low levels of hydrochloric acid, which causes physical symptoms of heartburn and gastric reflux. When there is not enough hydrochloric acid in our stomach then we are unable to effectively break down food into nutrients. There can also be poor absorption of nutrients in the small intestine caused by excess mucus buildup. Finally, there can be leaky gut syndrome where we do not breakdown food properly, and it creates an inflammatory process in the large intestine, often diagnosed as colitis or irritable bowel syndrome. All of these types of malabsorption can cause incomplete breakdown of proteins and fats, affecting brain communication that has been associated to restlessness, impulsiveness, and trouble learning.

Certain foods can cause these malabsorption problems. The first two foods to eliminate are casein, a milk protein, and gluten from wheat protein. These foods are used as fillers in many processed foods making it difficult to totally avoid them without thoroughly checking labels. I recommend staying off of all milk and dairy, and avoiding all gluten for at least two weeks to see what effect this has on digestion and thinking ability. If symptoms improve, then gradually add back one food at a time every week and watch your symptoms for a reoccurrence. By doing this with a number of foods you can find out what foods are truly affecting you. This takes time but will help you realize what you can eat and what foods cause you to have symptoms.

Also by making sure you are getting a full complement of nutrients, you should be able to reduce these food sensitivities. When certain B-vitamins and minerals are missing from our diet, we are more prone to wheat, citrus, and dairy allergies. As your health improves, and you get the nutrients your body requires, many of these food sensitivities will disappear as long as they do not get a chance to build up in your system again.

# Can Supplements Really Help?

Supplementing specific vitamins and other essential nutrients often helps control or improve behavior. We will look at four areas of nutrients that help improve health. First, we will look at the importance of getting B-complex vitamins in your diet or in daily supplements to reduce nervous system stress and improve metabolism. Then we will look at the role of antioxidants, minerals, amino acids, and essential fatty acid foods and supplements.

## B-Complex Vitamins

All of the B-complex vitamins are grouped together in many nutritional formulas since they are commonly found in the same foods. They also work together to balance metabolism, improve nervous system function, and support the immune and circulatory system. Symptoms related to B-complex vitamin deficiency are often looked at as stress related, such as headaches, anxiety, moodiness, and heart arrhythmias, and are often affected by excess sugar or alcohol in the diet. Since the B-complex vitamins are water soluble, they need to be replenished daily. People who eat a lot of sugar, drink alcohol, vegetarians, and people with malabsorption problems are the most prone to B-complex vitamin deficiencies.

A double-blind study was published in 1979 in the Journal of Biological Psychiatry showing that adding higher doses of vitamin B-6 to the diet can have a similar or better effect to taking Ritalin for symptoms of hyperactivity. **Vitamin B-6** is involved in building the immune system and metabolizing proteins and carbohydrates. It is found in brown rice, fish, butter, wheat germ, whole grain foods, and soybeans. Lack of Vitamin B-6 may result in neuropathy, insomnia, mental confusion and skin disorders such as acne or cracked lips.

Folic acid (B-9) and Vitamin B-12 are B-complex vitamins, which are very important for the circulatory system, and the prevention of nervous system damage. **Folic acid** is primarily found in green leafy vegetables and whole grains, and **Vitamin B-12** is found primarily in meats and eggs. Combined deficiency of vitamin B-12 and folic acid are not uncommon. Symptoms of these deficiencies are heart failure, skin weakness, pernicious anemia, with impaired digestion of food, nerve degeneration, muscular weakness, and dizziness.

Vitamin B-12 is also very important for our nervous system, and is needed to create and repair our DNA. Vitamin B-12 is absorbed best when combined with intrinsic factor, a protein made in the stomach. Since vitamin B-12 is found in protein foods, and not in any vegetable sources, vegetarians can easily become deficient in vitamin B-12.

**Niacin, vitamin B-3**, is also important for the nervous and digestive system. It is needed for keeping the skin healthy as well. Niacin is found in meat, fish, brewer's yeast, milk, eggs, legumes, and peanuts. Niacin needs to have the amino acid tryptophan in the diet when taken as a supplement to be absorbed well. If too much niacin is taken at once there can be flushing of the skin because it dilates the blood vessels, and overdoses can also cause headaches, cramps and itching. This reaction only lasts for a short time after taking high doses, and is not dangerous, but also is not recommended to do regularly.

**Pantothenic acid, vitamin B-5**, helps to reduce cortisol levels caused by stressed adrenals, and is often combined with vitamin B-6 in specific supplements for cortisol reduction. **Biotin** is another B-complex vitamin that works with pantothenic acid to create energy from carbohydrates. Dermatitis is a skin disorder seen by with a deficiency of biotin. Biotin is found in egg yolk, brewer's yeast, beef liver, peanuts, cauliflower and mushrooms.

## Antioxidants

**Vitamin C** is the best-known antioxidant vitamin. As a single antioxidant it does a lot to help in healing tissues and maintaining the integrity of the small blood vessels. There are three main vitamins that are classified as antioxidants, and some minerals. The other antioxidant vitamins are vitamin E, and Vitamin A often made from the plant chemical called beta carotene. The minerals that function as antioxidants are zinc and selenium. Other plant chemicals found in fruits, vegetables, and herbs, also known as phytochemicals, act as antioxidants. We need anti-oxidants to counteract free radicals created by our lifestyle, our metabolism, any bacteria, virus or fungus we have, and from mental / emotional stress. Every time we breathe, or eat, or exercise, we create dangerous free radicals that antioxidants have to destroy. Free radicals cause damage to our healthy cells, causing faster aging, and making us prone to more chronic disease conditions.

Antioxidants work best together. For example, taking just **vitamin E** alone can be dangerous because vitamin E becomes its own free radical after it kills off other free radicals. So vitamin C has to come in and kill off the vitamin E free radical. Every antioxidant works better with other antioxidants in a synergistic manner. Your immune system will function much better with antioxidants from a variety of fruits and vegetables instead of high doses of just one.

## Minerals

**Minerals** help to keep the nervous system in balance. Calcium and magnesium are the two major minerals that our body needs on a regular basis. **Calcium** is not just for our bones; it plays a vital role in improving nerve impulse contraction, releasing neurotransmitters, regulating blood pressure, and activating cell enzymes for energy production. **Magnesium** is the muscle-relaxing mineral that works with enzymes to create energy in our body. Many people who feel stressed, or are in chronic pain, are deficient in magnesium.

**Zinc** is essential to the normal structure and function of cells, especially in the brain. Zinc is an essential mineral that helps get rid of free radicals, provides nutritional support for teeth, bones, hair, nails and skin, is needed by thyroid and adrenal hormones, and is helpful for short term memory problems. **Copper** is the mineral that works with zinc to help maintain mental function and physical coordination. Too much copper will affect how zinc is absorbed has been shown to cause some Attention Deficit Disorder symptoms.

Mineral deficiencies affect the nervous system. When there is restless sleep, and daytime fatigue look for calcium and magnesium deficiencies. It is best to get minerals from whole foods, found mostly in vegetables. When you are not able to get enough vegetables you may need to supplement. Do not use just any mineral supplement. Make sure it has a full balance of minerals. It should have **calcium** with **magnesium** in a 2 to 1 ratio, or twice as many milligrams of calcium as magnesium. It also should have many of the **trace minerals**, such as zinc, selenium, manganese, silicon and boron. All of these minerals work with calcium to help it get absorbed better by the bones and nervous system. And since minerals work better with B-complex vitamins it is even better to get a supplement that contains both minerals and B-complex vitamins.

## Amino Acids and Neurotransmitters

In the first section, we talked about neurotransmitters and how they affect moods and behavior. Neurotransmitters help to create thoughts and sensations by creating chemical reactions in our brain. Each day we have billions of messages sent through our body to our brain using these neurotransmitters.

Specific neurotransmitters create a variety of feelings in our body. We can be happy or sad, energetic or depressed, wide-awake or sleepy depending on the amount of each neurotransmitter. The types of foods we eat daily, along with when we eat them, and how they are combined makes a difference in our neurotransmitter levels. Here we will look at how amino acids work with certain types of nutrients to affect neurotransmitter levels.

Amino acids are naturally derived from protein foods. There are 22 amino acids, and some of them are essential, meaning we have to supplement them in our diet, others are non-essential amino acids, meaning that we can make them from other amino acids or nutrients. Amino acids help battle fatigue by breaking down protein in the diet, so that energy levels and muscle strength improve more quickly. For mental energy you can increase the amount of high protein foods in your diet, that can be broken down into specific amino acids during digestion.

**Glutamic acid** and **glutamine** are amino acids that are needed for metabolism of nutrients for the brain. Glutamic acid activates the brain cells, is needed to detoxify ammonia free radicals, and helps maintain blood sugar levels. It works with other amino acids, like glutamine to keep the brain cells functioning effectively. Glutamine is another brain neurotransmitter that is also used to treat alcoholism and can help protect against alcohol poisoning. It also has been used effectively to treat senility and schizophrenia.

Biochemically, symptoms of Attention Deficit Disorder with hyperactivity are most likely caused by a deficiency in **dopamine**, the natural "feel-good" neurotransmitter. Dopamine is used to activate the frontal lobe of the brain found in the forehead area. This area of the brain is the decision-making area, and is in charge of bringing together thoughts, feelings, and sensory information. The frontal lobe compiles information that helps determine daily objectives and results. So it is not surprising when dopamine activity is out of balance, someone can have trouble concentrating and staying focused.

There are a variety of factors that can cause dopamine deficiency. A stressful lifestyle, nutritional deficiencies and toxins in the environment all are factors, along with some genetic tendencies, that can affect how dopamine is processed in the brain.

One amino acid, called **tyrosine**, increases the production of the neurotransmitters dopamine and norepinephrine. **Tyrosine** is processed from the essential amino acid **phenylalanine** to create norepinephrine and dopamine. Tyrosine is an amino acid that is needed by the adrenal, pituitary and thyroid glands. It helps generates red and white blood cells for the immune system. It can be used to improve mood, deepen sleep and reduce anxiety and depression. It helps produce melanin needed to maintain color in the hair and skin. It is one of the most important amino acids used for Attention Deficit Disorder since it increases the production of both norepinephrine and dopamine that are needed to increase levels of alertness and energy. You find tyrosine in high protein foods including fish, poultry, meat, and eggs.

**Phenylalanine** is an essential amino acid that helps produce and maintain a positive mood, and improve alertness and ambition. It can enhance learning and memory since it helps produce dopamine and norepinephrine that control impulse transmission between nerve cells. Along with other amino acids it is commonly used for depression and to suppress appetite. Some people who have a genetic impairment are not able to convert phenylalanine to tyrosine, which can cause some forms of mental retardation. Then tyrosine can become an essential amino acid to be supplemented as needed.

Amino acids do not work alone. They often depend on other vitamins and minerals to be more effective. **Vitamin C** is needed to help tyrosine and phenylalanine make dopamine and norepinephrine. Adding additional vitamin C to the diet may be an easy way of improving norepinephrine levels when there are adequate protein levels.

**Acetylcholine** is the neurotransmitter that controls your parasympathetic nervous system. This means that it helps the digestive process, regulates breathing, and slows the heart rate. Acetylcholine helps your body relax, and is used up more when you are under a lot of stress. Your body will make its own acetylcholine from choline. **Choline** is available in the diet as phosphatidylcholine, found in lecithin. Choline is a B-complex vitamin that is found in protein foods, especially in eggs. Choline is used to make the neurotransmitter acetylcholine, needed for memory and concentration.

**Lecithin** is a structural material found in every cell in the body. It is an essential component of the human brain and nervous system. It forms 30 percent of the dry weight of the brain and 17 percent of the nervous system. Lecithin is a supplement that is a major source of choline. Besides being needed for mental acuity, lecithin helps the body burn fat, lowers blood cholesterol, and improves vitamin E absorption. Lecithin can be taken as a daily supplement and is safe when between 600 mg or to 2400 mg is taken per day as a powder or soft gel. Lecithin is found mostly in egg yolks, and in smaller quantities in whole milk, meat, soybeans, and whole grains.

Also your body can make its own lecithin. But it needs a good quantity of B-complex vitamins, especially B-6 (pyridoxine) for this to occur. B-6 deficiency is very common in Americans. The RDA is only 2 milligrams, but with our stressful lifestyle, at least 50 to 100 mg per day is often required. If you get too much B-6, usually over 2000 milligrams per day you will experience numbness or tingling in your arms and legs.

**Serotonin** is a calming neurotransmitter that can decrease hypersensitivity, and reduce appetite, yet in too high an amount will cause depression and excess sleep. This is the amino acid that is reduced during low carbohydrate diets, causing symptoms of depression. Nutritionally, serotonin levels are supported by sufficient amounts of vitamin B-6, folic acid, niacin, iron and vitamin C.

The amino acid **tryptophan** is used to produce serotonin. Tryptophan is known as the calming amino acid, and it is found in turkey, chicken, nuts, beans and some dairy products. By getting more tryptophan in your diet, you will produce more serotonin and be able to sleep better. Tryptophan is also helpful for reducing migraine headaches.

You can also create more serotonin by getting sufficient amounts of niacin, or vitamin B-3. Tryptophan is broken down into niacin, and so if you supplement with at least 50 mg of niacin per day you may be able to relax better and sleep more soundly. Of course, too much niacin can cause a warm flushing or tingling effect on your skin.

Serotonin is the neurotransmitter that is increased by eating carbohydrates. When there is hyperactivity or excess stress, carbohydrates help to get more insulin into the bloodstream. Insulin will clear out excess amino acids in the blood, except tryptophan.

This is one reason to avoid eating proteins and carbohydrates at the same meal. To maintain a more balanced neurotransmitter state, it is beneficial to eat proteins with low carbohydrate foods during the day when you want to be more alert, and carbohydrate snacks at other times of the day when you need to calm down.

I do not recommend supplementing with specific amino acids until all other nutritional factors are addressed. Just get a balanced amount of protein daily.

### Essential Fatty Acids

Purdue University researchers found in a June 1996 study that boys with low blood levels of essential omega-3 fatty acids have a greater tendency to have problems with behavior and learning, related to Attention Deficit Hyperactivity Disorder.

If you have dry skin, stiffness, concentration problems, or hormonal imbalances you may be lacking in a type of fat that is essential to health. Essential fatty acids are those fats that the body needs; yet cannot synthesize itself. Fatty acids are the building blocks of fats. Although many types of fat are unhealthy fats, some are beneficial and necessary. In fact, cutting all fat from the diet is actually harmful to your health.

Essential fatty acids are crucial in the proper metabolism of fats. Yet, the standard American diet mainly consists of fats that are deficient in these essential nutrients. Saturated fat is one type of harmful fat that is found in many types of red meat and dairy foods. Partially hydrogenated oils that are most commonly found in snack foods are even more detrimental to health. These types of fats, found in most processed vegetable oils, are converted to trans-fatty acids when heated, or oxidized. These are the types of fat that increase cholesterol in the arteries. These trans-fatty acids cannot be assimilated by the body, and are linked to many negative and serious health conditions, such as heart disease and cancer.

Essential fatty acids are important in many metabolic processes, including energy production. Since the body cannot produce them, they must be consumed in the diet to optimize health. The essential fatty acids are the omega-3 (linoleic) and omega-6 (linolenic) fatty acids. These nutrients are the main structural components of the body's cell membranes, are crucial to optimum performance, and can enhance overall health if they are present in adequate quantities. Omega-3 and omega-6 are also important in preventing damage from other fats.

Omega-3 and omega-6 are the two polyunsaturated fatty acids that are necessary to produce prostaglandins, hormone-like substances, which regulate many functions in the body. Prostaglandins control every cell in the body and are required for energy production. Prostaglandins increase the metabolic rate and stamina, and decrease recovery time from fatigue. Essential fatty acids help to form the structural part of all cell membranes, regulate the flow of substances into and out of the cells, and protect the cells from invading bacteria, viruses, allergens, and other toxins. Essential fatty acids are especially needed for proper brain functioning.

Every cell in the body is like a tiny factory, taking in raw materials from the surrounding fluid and sending out various chemicals. Everything going into or coming out of the cell has to pass through the cell's membrane. The membrane depends on essential fatty acids to remain fluid and flexible. Without them, the membrane becomes stiff and unable to do its job.

Essential fatty acids are also important in oxygen transfer and red blood cell production. They shorten recovery time from fatigue since they encourage the blood to bring vital oxygen to muscle cells and they enable the cells to more easily absorb nutrients needed for recuperation.

This is a list of the benefits realized by getting of essential fatty acids in your diet:

- Improved cholesterol levels
- Lower blood pressure
- Improved memory

- Increased circulation
- Reduced joint stiffness
- Reduced dryness of the skin
- Improved immune system function
- Less inflammation
- Balanced hormones
- Depression reduced.

As you can see, fatty acids are essential for metabolism and health. There are two **omega-3** essential fatty acids called eicosapentaenoic acid (EPA) and docosaheaenoic acid (DHA) found in cold-water fish and other northern marine animals. There are also plant sources of precursors to essential fatty acids EPA and DHA. Flax seed, hemp, walnut and soybean oil contain an omega-3 essential fatty acid called alpha-linolenic acid (ALA), which can be converted through several stages into EPA and then into DHA.

**Flax oil** is the richest natural plant source of omega-3 fats. It contains 57% omega-3 fatty acid and 16% omega-6 fatty acid. It is commonly used in salads in place of other salad dressing oils. Flax oil shouldn't be used for cooking, as high heat damages the fatty acids. The other main sources of omega-3 fatty acids are fish oils from salmon, tuna, cod, and mackerel.

**Omega-6** fatty acids are found in many vegetable oils such as borage, flaxseed, walnut, soy, corn, sunflower, and are especially abundant in evening primrose oil. These omega-6 acids are the precursors of gamma linolenic acid (GLA). Supplements providing GLA, such as primrose oil, helps the body make prostaglandins, the substances that help to relax muscles that tend to cramp, and keep the skin more moist.

Both omega-3 and omega-6 fatty acids need to be supplemented in the diet. The ideal ratio of these fats for healthy people is 2 parts omega-6 to 1 part omega-3. Since more omega-6 is used in the common diet of Americans, this ratio is often out of balance by as much as 6:1. For people who have immune system weakness, heart disease, or blood sugar imbalances, there is a need to increase the amount of omega-3 fats so that the prostaglandins can get into a better balance. Increasing the amount of fish oils and flax oil will help get the omega-3 fatty acids into the cell membranes to balance prostaglandins. 2000 mg. of flax oil is usually equivalent to 2 capsules or 1 tablespoon, and is the recommended minimum per day.

The omega-3 and omega-6 need catalysts to be absorbed in the body. These catalysts are vitamins B-3 (niacin) and B-6, vitamin C, and the minerals magnesium and zinc. When these nutrients are not sufficient then the essential fatty acids will not be absorbed well. Also when too many saturated or trans fats are part of the normal diet then supplementation of essential fatty acids is less effective.

Find a way to get these essential fatty acids in your diet daily. Adjust the types of fats your family eats. Add good fats such as olive oil to cooked vegetables, or use flax oil as the oil in your homemade salad dressing. Limit all trans fats, or anything with partially hydrogenated oils. Eat more fish, especially cold-water fish like salmon. Or you can take daily supplements that usually are in soft gel form. Some people experience burping or tasting fish when taking **fish oil soft gels**. Keeping the supplement refrigerated so that the soft gel is cold enough to breakdown later in the digestive tract can prevent this reaction.

The brain is 20% fat and these essential fatty acids fulfill very important functions in preventing many mental and physical conditions. The myelin sheath that surrounds our brain cells contains essential fatty acids that are directly involved in receptor formation and nerve transmission. We need to make sure we are getting more good or essential fats in our diet than bad trans fats. This will help with nutrient absorption and improve our brain function and regeneration. As we age it is even more important to get these good fats to prevent many of the neurological diseases we fear today, such as Alzheimer's or Parkinson's Disease. A Harvard study recently found that people using EPA and DHA fish oil supplements had better control of bipolar depression than those using psychiatric medications. Since similar results are found for Attention Deficit Disorder, there is no age limit on using omega-3 fish oils or flax oils on a daily basis.

## So Which Supplements Are Best to Take?

In the next chapter we are going to look at the benefit of whole food supplements. Supplements that contain whole foods will have the components that your body recognizes, and so will have less of a possibility of increasing stress on your system. When buying nutritional supplements it is best to get a good combination of:

**Antioxidants** – Vitamins A (beta carotene, alpha carotene) Vitamin C, Vitamin E, green tea, grapeseed extract, milk thistle, alpha lipoic acid.

**Minerals** – Calcium with magnesium (2:1 ratio), along with zinc, copper, manganese, chromium, selenium, silicon and boron.

**B-Vitamin Complex** – with all the B-vitamins included especially folic acid, and vitamin B-6 and B-12.

**Enzymes** – digestive enzymes that help your body digest the foods you eat – amylase for carbohydrates, protease for protein foods, lipase for fat digestion, and cellulase for fiber digestion. Also pepsin is an additional enzyme that helps breakdown foods better in the stomach.

**Essential Fatty Acids** – 1000 to 2000 milligrams of omega-3 fish oil or flax oil per day. Plus 500 to 1000 milligrams of omega-6 Evening Primrose Oil or borage oil per day.

Whole foods that are commonly added to vitamin and mineral supplements are broccoli powder, carrot powder, and garlic. **Herbs** are also added to many supplements instead of common foods. Some of the common herbs that are added are milk thistle and turmeric, which assist the liver in metabolizing the other ingredients in the supplement. Green foods are also added to supplements, such as spirulina, and lecithin to provide chlorophyll and minerals.

I would not recommend buying separate containers of each of these components. It easier on your system to take a supplement with antioxidants, minerals, B-complex vitamins, and enzymes combined. Make sure it has some digestive enzymes, and has some food powders, herbs, or green foods to help your body absorb the nutrients easier.

I also recommend that you get your antioxidants, minerals and enzymes supplements in capsules. Too often tablets are hard to digest and do not breakdown in your system soon enough to have all the nutrients absorbed. When looking at liquid vitamin and minerals supplements, make sure it does not contain any sugar in the form of sucrose or fructose. Sweeteners that are added will rob the supplement of nutrients, especially of B-vitamins, and so will not be as effective.

Then you can add a few soft gels of essential fatty acids and your body will be getting the supplementation it needs on daily basis.

# *Benefits of Whole Food Supplements*

When recommending supplements to children and adults with Attention Deficit Disorder, or for those who just want to feel healthier on a daily basis, I like to look for the simplest things that they can do. If they are having trouble thinking clearly, they will probably have trouble remembering to take many supplements. Also, when the body is stressed, the adrenal glands do better with fewer supplements that need to be assimilated. So I look for supplements that have all the nutrients that work together. This is why I first recommend whole food supplements to my clients.

I recommend whole food supplements that contain a variety of fruits and vegetables. The different colors in each fruit and vegetable are one representation of the **phytochemicals**, or beneficial plant chemicals, that are found in them. For example, lycopene, a phytochemical found in tomatoes and other red fruits and vegetables, is the pigment that makes a tomato red. Lycopene is necessary to prevent prostate problems, and reduce the effects of sun damage on the skin.

Green fruits and vegetables are especially good for the circulatory system. There are many green vegetables such as broccoli, spinach, parsley, kale, Brussels sprouts, and asparagus. They contain many minerals and B-complex vitamins. Two of the phytochemicals found in green foods are sulforaphane and indoles that are very powerful anti-cancer compounds. Researchers have tried to use these as isolated phytochemicals but find that they only work well in the whole food form.

Orange foods have the carotenoids that help prevent cancer by repairing the DNA. Some of the more beneficial orange vegetables are carrots, pumpkin, and squash. As our mothers told us, carrots, as well as any other orange foods, are especially good for our eyes, and help with night vision. These deep orange foods help our body get the vitamin A we need, without getting excess that can lead to osteoporosis.

Fruits and vegetables that are in the blue and purple color group are very rich in powerful antioxidants called anthocyanins that protect again heart disease by improving circulation and preventing blood clots. Blue and purple fruits that contain anthocyanins are Concord grapes, blueberries, blackberries, along with dark red raspberries. They also have many anti-aging phytochemicals that keep the blood circulating, thereby reducing the effects of the Standard American Diet that is rich in trans fats and processed foods.

Getting a variety of different colors in our daily diet will provide us with these phytochemical nutrients that we cannot get in vitamin and mineral supplements. Our immune system will work better, our internal stress level will go down, and our liver will be able to detoxify free radicals from our system better. When our liver functions better we will have a happier outlook on life, we will have less headaches, and we will not get irritable or angry as easily. Stress on our liver can cause emotional swings related to metabolism problems and toxic buildup from food additives.

Getting a variety of fruits and vegetables is important because they each contain thousands of different phytochemicals, or plant chemicals, that work together as antioxidants, minerals, enzymes, and essential fatty acids to help improve our health. There are no vitamin or mineral supplements in any store that contains all the nutrients found in fruits and vegetables. So how do we get them in our diet? Now thanks to modern production techniques we are able to encapsulate fruits and vegetables without losing their nutritional quality.

**Nutraceuticals** are nutritional supplements that have been tested and proven to help improve health. They are dietary substances that have concentrated nutrition levels that provide more benefit than the food can by itself. Depending on how a supplement is processed it can become a nutraceutical.

One way of concentrating the nutrition from fruits and vegetables is by juicing them. If you juice a whole pound of carrots, you get about 8 ounces of carrot juice. Most of the fiber is lost when juicing, but the nutrient quality goes up because the juice contains most of the nutrients. Also you can drink more juice than you can eat when the vegetable is in its whole form. When this juice is dried into a powder with the water taken out, you get a highly concentrated food powder. This is an example of concentrated whole food nutrition that can be encapsulated. The nutritional quality is maintained and cumulative healthy effects are seen when these nutritional supplements are taken over time.

When choosing a whole food supplement look at how the foods are combined. In juicing we are told not to combine fruits and vegetables together. Exceptions are that apples can go in vegetable juices and carrots can be mixed in fruit juices. Yet fruits and vegetables have different functions in improving our health, and ideally should not be mixed together in a supplement. This is why I recommend **Juice Plus+®** to my clients as the best choice of a whole food based product. Juice Plus+® separates the fruit and vegetable capsules into two bottles to be taken at different times of the day.

There is a Children's Health Study going on right now, looking at the effects of consistently taking **Juice Plus+®,** a whole food based product, containing the nutritional essence of 7 fruits and 10 vegetables and grains. It is an ongoing study measuring various improvements in health after one year of supplementation. The study is aimed at helping children's health improve, but families are filling out the questionnaire to evaluate the benefits realized by everyone who is participating. For every child on Juice Plus+®, a corresponding adult is also taking Juice Plus+®. This way the parents and children are involved together in establishing good health habits. The following table shows the positive effects on children and adults when using Juice Plus+®.

| After one full year on Juice Plus+® | Children | Adults |
|---|---|---|
| Eating less fast food/ fewer soft drinks | 61% | 64% |
| Eating more fruits and vegetables | 43% | 59% |
| Fewer doctor visits | 46% | 32% |
| Taking less prescription drugs | 26% | 14% |
| Taking less over-the counter medication | 34% | 22% |
| Less school or work missed | 39% | 35% |
| Positive benefit of some kind | 90% | 85% |
| Increased awareness of health | 80% | 82% |

# Section 3

# *Using Homeopathy for Attention Deficit Disorder*

# *Using Homeopathy for Attention Deficit Disorder*

## Quick Find Outline

Understanding Homeopathy

Symptoms to find a Homeopathic Remedy

# *Understanding Homeopathy*

Homeopathy is a medical science that uses microdoses of substances to create a natural healing response. Even though many medical professionals do not understand how it can work, testimonials from satisfied clients are making homeopathic remedies more common in our retail stores. People often learn about homeopathy from friends and colleagues who have used it successfully in the past. They are looking for safe alternatives that will not create future health problems, and that really look at the underlying cause of the current symptoms.

Homeopathy is a very safe alternative to conventional medicines for Attention Deficit Disorder, and is much more inexpensive to use. Also, it is not long-term therapy. A homeopathic remedy does not suppress symptoms; it actually reverses stress that is causing the symptoms to manifest. After choosing a matching remedy, the remedy is taken for a short period of time, and then the symptoms are re-evaluated. Often other health symptoms improve along with the behavior problems. Since each homeopathic remedy works on the whole body – mind, head, face, chest, back, stomach, abdomen, legs, arms, and even sleep patterns, when you use the proper remedy, other physical symptoms will also get better.

Many children have seen dramatic improvements after homeopathic treatment. The same is true for adults with many focus and concentration problems ranging from learning disabilities, depression, anxiety, phobias, and Obsessive-Compulsive Disorder.

Homeopathic remedies are made from plants, minerals, or animals in very small doses to stimulate the sick person's natural defenses. The most basic principle of homeopathy is called the **Law of Similars**, or "like cures like." This principle dates back to the fourth century B.C. when the philosopher Hippocrates treated diseases with similar substances. In the 15th century, Paracelsus, a physician who studied herbs, also used the Law of Similars in using the herb hellebore, which usually causes diarrhea in high doses, to cure diarrhea when given in a very small dose. The theory states that small doses of a specific substance will help cure symptoms that can be caused by an overdose or over use of the same substance. Take for instance, the symptoms of a sore throat, which include burning and stinging pain with redness and some swelling. These are very similar to bee sting symptoms. In homeopathy, Apis mellifica is a remedy made from a honeybee. It can be used to reverse the effects of bee stings, sore throats, and any other symptoms that include burning and stinging pain with redness and swelling, like sunburn.

The name homeopathy comes from the Greek "Homeo" meaning *similar* and "pathos" meaning *disease* or *suffering*. The remedies are used to stimulate the client's natural healing ability, and do not work to control symptoms. This Law of Similars, the basic principle of homeopathy, is comparable to immunizations and allergy treatments used in conventional medicine. Yet, allergy treatments and immunizations are not given in small enough amounts to truly be a homeopathic dose.

The two other principles of homeopathy, after the **Law of Similars**, are the Law of Individualization and the Law of the Minimum Dose. The **Law of Individualization** indicates that each person should be treated based on his or her own specific symptoms, not on generalized symptoms. For example, there are many symptoms of a headache. By looking at the location of the head pain, the type of pain, and what makes the pain worse or better, we can find the specific remedy that matches the symptoms. Homeopaths recognize that symptoms are our body's signal that there is something wrong. Whether is it pain or anxiety, our symptoms try to communicate to us what is out of balance. It is our responsibility to recognize these symptoms, and not suppress them with drugs. It is much better in the long term to stimulate a true healing response so that the stress that is causing the symptoms is gone, rather than having the body continue to deal with the stress that comes with suppressed symptoms.

The third principle, the **Law of the Minimum Dose**, recommends the use of the smallest dose possible to create a healing reaction. This is why homeopathic remedies are prepared in diluted doses. Samuel Hahnemann created a two-step process that dilutes substances into microdoses. The two steps are dilution and succession. Succussion is done by shaking the remedy vigorously between each dilution process. Each time the substance is diluted, less of the original substance exists, and so the deeper the remedy works to heal the body. Sometimes the substance becomes so diluted that none of the original substance is left, only a magnetic memory remains in the liquid remedy, and yet it still works to help heal specific symptoms.

Since the homeopathic remedies are in such diluted forms, if you take a remedy that does not fit your symptoms well, you will not see a healing response, yet you will not get side effects either. So they are generally regarded as a safer alternative than using herbs that can cause side effects when used incorrectly. Homeopathic remedies are acknowledged by the FDA as "over-the-counter drugs" and so are available to buy in many health food and some regular retail stores.

## History of Homeopathy

A German physician, named Samuel Hahnemann, developed homeopathy in the early 1800's. Dr. Hahnemann was translating a medical book when he discovered homeopathic principles. He decided to try some self-made remedies on himself and on his acquaintances. As each substance was tested and found to be effective, Dr. Hahnemann created documentation of homeopathic remedies and uses, and made the remedies available to medical doctors.

Homeopathy became popular in Europe and in the United States due to its success in treating the epidemics during the late 1800's. Diseases, such as cholera, yellow fever, and scarlet fever were some of the infectious diseases that were treated successfully using homeopathic remedies. The death rate was reduced over 50% in people using homeopathic remedies versus conventional therapies.

By the early 1900's, one out of six medical doctors in the United States used homeopathic remedies. At the turn of the century, 15% of doctors specialized in homeopathy. Large medical universities like the University of Michigan, and University of California – Los Angeles graduated homeopathic doctors. In the early 1900's the American Medical Association, run by conventional doctors, felt seriously threatened by homeopathic doctors, and applied pressure on them by limiting funding sources to the universities that had homeopathic schools. So even though the popularity of homeopathy was misplaced in the United States for a few decades, it continued to be used in other parts of the world.

Right now, about 40% of the people in France use homeopathic remedies recommended by their doctors. In Germany, about 20% of the doctors there use homeopathic remedies, and in South America it is also very popular. It is also very common in England where the royal family has benefited from using homeopathy for over 100 years. India has the most homeopathic medical schools and many of the homeopathic reference books originated in India. Within the last 15 years there has been a 35% to 50% increase in the sales of homeopathic remedies in the United States. Patients who used to leave the country to get homeopathic remedies began requesting that they become available in the United States too, and this has led to the revival of homeopathy in America.

## Homeopathic Symptom Profiles

When you go to a homeopathic practitioner be prepared to tell them about your very specific symptoms, since a successful homeopathic remedy is chosen after a detailed questioning process. The homeopath will ask you many questions about your physical symptoms, your mental state, your likes and dislikes, your fears, your eating habits and anything else that might help in forming your personal profile. The homeopath will then match your profile to one of the hundreds of remedy pictures listed in the homeopathic book called the Materia Medica.

Each individual is unique, and it is that exclusive pattern that makes using homeopathic remedies different than conventional medicine. Homeopathic doctors always take the whole person into account. If the chief complaint of the person is his inability to sit still, difficulty concentrating, or other symptoms of ADD, these behaviors will be recorded, but in combination with the person's other symptoms. The homeopath notes anything unusual about that person. That might include past historical events in their life, fears they have and have not dealt with, food cravings, and dream patterns. By listing at least 10 to 15 specific mental and physical symptoms of the individual, the homeopath can find the remedy that matches their symptom and personality pattern.

By finding the most specific homeopathic remedy, both physical ailments and emotional upsets can be reversed. Also when homeopathic remedies are used, people tend to feel less stressed and more energized. Instead of suppressing the excess energy in hyperactive children, they are able to use their energy in constructive ways. When they are able to direct their own ambitions they will feel more successful in life, and their self-esteem will improve.

## Attention Deficit Symptoms in Homeopathy

Homeopathic remedies help people with Attention Deficit Disorder by reducing the stresses that are causing the mental, emotional and physical symptoms being displayed. Finding the homeopathic remedy that specifically matches the unique symptoms of the individual will stimulate a healing response that will feel like a burden has been lifted. This shows up as a more balanced condition depending on the need of the body to either calm down, or to get more energetic. It is very important to find the best homeopathic remedy that matches the client's symptoms. That is why it is crucial to learn as much as possible about the client's symptom picture. I usually ask people to bring in a list of their symptoms written down. I look for behavioral symptoms – their overall personality, how they learn, what their temper is like, what are they afraid of, and how they interact in social situations. I also look at physical symptoms – a common pattern to illness, what usually makes them feel better, and their sleep patterns.

For parents of children with Attention Deficit Disorder I like to get the parents list of their child's symptoms, and then watch and interview the child during the appointment. Children often are sensitive to being "talked about" and so I like to get their perspective of their life. I look at the child's response to me, to the things in my office, to their parents when answering questions, and to their parent's response when I ask their parents questions about them. I have a box of toys in the office for children to play with. This shows me how they organize their environment, and how they interact with their parents and me. These toys also show me how their parents interact with them. I have watched parents tell their children what to do with each toy, not allowing the child to play using their own imagination, creating more stress in the child's life.

Looking at body language during the interview can help discover different mannerisms that are commonly found in homeopathic remedy profiles. When children have specific habits like picking their nose, having to touch everything in sight, squinting, or scratching certain areas of their body, these gestures need to be noted. They are often listed in remedy profiles.

When children come in with their parents, and depending on the child's age, the way the child responds to me can make a big difference in choosing the best remedy. For example, when the child basically tries to hide from me during the office visit, even after realizing that I am not going to touch them, that can indicate one remedy profile. Then there is the child who answers all of the questions whether asked to them or not, and wants to be the center of attention, indicates another personality profile.

### Types of Homeopathic Remedies
Different types of homeopathic remedies are found in health food stores and offices of homeopathic doctors. Classical homeopathy uses one substance made from a plant, mineral, or animal that has been proven to reverse certain symptom patterns. **Classical remedies** usually come in small lactose sugar pellets that have been saturated with a liquid remedy. A classical remedy is chosen by taking a complete physical and mental health history; then consulting a homeopathic repertory book or computer program, to find the remedy that matches the most symptoms. Classical remedies work very well when they are well chosen.

It is recognized in homeopathy that certain people fit into a very specific personality type that matches both their physical and mental symptoms. This is referred to in homeopathy as a "**Constitutional Type**". By recording a detailed profile of the a person's health history, current and reoccurring health challenges, personal likes and dislikes, and mental and emotional patterns and sensitivities we can begin to match them to a number of common remedies used in homeopathy. The constitutional remedy chosen will be the best match to most of their symptoms.

Constitutional remedies are used more often when there are chronic problems or when mental / emotional symptoms are being displayed. They are very useful in choosing a remedy for Attention Deficit Disorder after noting the specific symptoms of the child or adult. The constitutional type is named after a specific remedy, and addresses the various physical, emotional, and mental problems that it clears.

When a person is experiencing an acute illness like a cold or injury, then it is more common to use another type of remedy for the current health challenge. The homeopathic medicines found in most health food stores are called "**combination remedies**" since they have a number of low potency remedies combined together. On average a combination remedy will have between three to eight different homeopathic substances mixed together. The various manufacturers choose the low potency remedies that are most commonly prescribed for specific symptoms and assume that one or more of them will help cure the ailment that the consumer has.

These combination remedies are popular in health food stores because they often work well, and it does not take a long time to find the right remedy. Also, since these medicines are much safer than conventional drugs, they are generally preferable to a growing number of consumers. Combination remedies are usually in a much lower potency than classical remedies, so they usually need to be taken more often. Combination remedies are invaluable, but most professional homeopaths have found that the classical remedy individually chosen for each person tends to be more successful in stimulating long-term healing.

# *Symptoms to Find A Homeopathic Remedy*

## Homeopathic Personality Profiles Chart

Choosing the right classical remedy for a client is much easier when we can use a chart of symptoms that are matched up to symptoms associated with homeopathic remedies. Many different homeopathic remedy charts have been created for various health conditions. Here we will be using a homeopathic remedy chart specifically designed to use with Attention Deficit Disorder. It contains many mental and emotional symptoms that correlate to each remedy along with specific symptoms found in Attention Deficit Disorder. The following chart has about 100 physical, mental, and emotional symptoms that are found in 24 different classical homeopathic remedies. This chart can be used to find a classical remedy that most closely matches a person's symptom profile.

To use the chart on the next four pages, I recommend that you first check off the symptoms on the left column that relate to the symptoms found in the person being evaluated. Then go across each row and circle the X's that relate to the checked symptom. Add up the total of X's in each column per page, and then the final total on the last page. Each remedy has about 8 to 10 symptoms related to it. At the bottom of the 4ᵗʰ page, when you get a grand total you can find the three remedies with the highest scores. Then you can compare those three remedies with the more detailed explanations that follow the chart.

These 24 classical remedies are some common constitutional remedies along with some specific remedies used for Attention Deficit Disorder symptoms. The remedies are in their Latin names; so do not worry if you cannot pronounce the name of the remedy. The common name is listed next to the Latin name in the remedy list that follows the chart.

The symptoms that are designated for each remedy have been chosen from the Materia Medica for homeopathic remedies. After this chart there is a written explanation of each remedy with a list of correlating symptoms. You can also go through that list and check off the symptoms that fit, and see if the two or three best remedies are the same from the homeopathic chart and the list of remedies. Sometimes there is a clear picture of a constitutional remedy and other times it is a little more vague. Consulting additional homeopathic resources in books and online can help you figure out which remedy is the best, if you still have questions.

## Symptoms of Homeopathic Remedies Chart

| Check if YES | Symptoms | Argentum nit. | Arsenicum alb. | Baryta carb. | Belladonna | Calcarea carb. | Calcarea phos. | Carcinosium | Chamomilla |
|---|---|---|---|---|---|---|---|---|---|
| | Adverse to touch | | | | | | | | |
| | Aggressive | | | | | | | | |
| | Angry | X | X | | X | | | | |
| | Backward | | | X | | | | | |
| | Bad temper | | | | | | | | X |
| | Boastful | | | | | | | | |
| | Can't cope with change | | | | | | | | |
| | Cautious | | | | | X | | | |
| | Changeable | | | | | | | | |
| | Class clown | | | X | | | | | |
| | Complaining | | | | | | | | X |
| | Craves chocolate | | | | | | | | |
| | Craves salty foods | | | | | | | | |
| | Craves sweets | X | | | | | | | |
| | Cruel to people | | | | | | | | |
| | Cruel to animals | | | | | | | | |
| | Crys easily | | | | | | | | |
| | Delayed social development | | X | | | | | | |
| | Delayed mental development | | X | | | | | | |
| | Delayed physical development | | X | | | | | | |
| | Depression | | | | | | | | |
| | Destructive | | | | | | | | |
| | Difficult thinking | X | | | | | | X | |
| | Disobedient | | | | | | | | |
| | Dyslexia | | | | | | | | |
| | Easily Discouraged | | | | | | | | |

## Symptoms of Homeopathic Remedies Chart (page 1)

| Cina | Hyoscamus | Ignatia | Lachesis | Lycopodium | Medorrhinum | Natrum mur. | Nux vomica | Phosphorus | Platina | Pulsatilla | Stramonium | Sulfur | Tarantula hisp. | Tuberculinum | Veratrum alb. |
|---|---|---|---|---|---|---|---|---|---|---|---|---|---|---|---|
| X |  |  |  |  |  | X |  |  |  |  |  |  |  |  |  |
|  |  |  |  |  |  |  |  |  |  |  | X |  |  |  |  |
|  |  |  |  |  |  |  | X |  |  |  |  |  |  |  |  |
|  |  |  |  |  |  |  |  |  |  |  |  |  |  |  |  |
|  |  |  |  |  |  |  |  |  |  |  |  |  |  |  |  |
|  |  |  |  | X |  |  | X |  |  |  |  |  |  |  |  |
|  |  |  |  | X |  |  |  |  |  |  |  |  |  |  |  |
|  |  |  |  |  |  |  |  |  |  |  |  |  |  |  |  |
|  |  | X |  |  |  |  |  |  |  | X |  |  |  |  |  |
|  |  |  |  |  |  |  |  |  |  |  |  | X |  |  |  |
|  |  |  |  | X |  |  |  |  |  |  |  |  |  |  |  |
|  |  |  |  | X |  |  |  |  |  |  |  |  |  |  |  |
|  |  |  |  |  |  | X |  |  |  |  |  |  |  |  |  |
| X |  |  |  |  |  |  |  |  |  |  |  |  |  |  |  |
|  |  |  |  |  |  |  |  |  | X |  |  |  |  |  |  |
|  |  |  |  |  |  |  |  |  |  |  |  |  |  | X |  |
|  |  | X |  |  |  |  |  |  |  | X |  |  |  |  |  |
|  |  |  |  |  |  |  |  |  |  |  |  |  |  |  |  |
|  |  |  |  |  |  |  |  |  |  |  |  |  |  |  |  |
|  |  |  |  |  |  |  |  |  |  |  |  |  |  |  |  |
|  |  |  | X |  |  | X |  |  |  |  |  |  |  |  |  |
|  |  |  |  |  |  |  |  |  |  |  |  |  | X | X | X |
|  |  |  | X |  |  |  |  |  |  |  |  |  |  |  |  |
| X |  |  |  |  |  |  |  |  |  |  |  |  |  |  |  |
|  |  |  |  | X |  |  |  |  |  |  |  |  |  |  |  |
|  |  |  |  |  |  |  |  |  |  | X |  |  |  |  |  |

## Symptoms of Homeopathic Remedies Chart

| Check if YES | Symptoms | Argentum nit. | Arsenicum alb. | Baryta carb. | Belladonna | Calcarea carb. | Calcarea phos. | Carcinosium | Chamomilla |
|---|---|---|---|---|---|---|---|---|---|
| | Egotistical | | | | | | | | |
| | Episodes of rage | | | | | | | | |
| | Fears - many | | | | | | X | X | |
| | Fear of being alone | | X | | | | | | |
| | Fear of being criticized | | | X | | | | | X |
| | Fear of being unloved | | | | | | | | |
| | Fear of dogs | | | | | X | | | |
| | Fear of failure | X | | | | | | | |
| | Fear of ghosts | | | | X | | | | |
| | Fear of heights | | | | | X | | | |
| | Fidgety | | | | | | | | X |
| | Forgetful | | | | X | | X | | |
| | Frustrated | | | | | | X | | X |
| | Hard to make friends | | | | | | | | |
| | High expectations | | | | | | | | |
| | Hits others | | | | | | | | |
| | Hurried | X | | | | | | | |
| | Hopelessness | | X | | | | | | |
| | Hyperactive | | X | | | | X | X | |
| | Hyperchrondrial | | X | | | | | | |
| | Impatient | X | | | X | | | | X |
| | Impulsive | X | | | | | | | |
| | Incompetent feelings | | | | | X | | | |
| | Indifferent | | | | | | | | |
| | Insecure | | | | | | | | |
| | Irritable | | | | | | | | |

## Symptoms of Homeopathic Remedies Chart (page 2)

| Cina | Hyoscamus | Ignatia | Lachesis | Lycopodium | Medorrhinum | Natrum mur. | Nux vomica | Phosphorus | Platina | Pulsatilla | Stramonium | Sulfur | Tarantula hisp. | Tuberculinum | Veratrum alb. |
|---|---|---|---|---|---|---|---|---|---|---|---|---|---|---|---|
|  |  |  |  |  |  |  | X |  |  |  |  | X |  |  |  |
|  | X |  |  |  |  |  |  |  | X |  |  |  |  |  |  |
|  |  |  |  |  |  |  |  |  |  |  | X |  |  |  |  |
|  |  |  |  |  |  |  |  | X |  | X |  |  | X |  |  |
|  |  |  |  | X |  |  |  |  |  |  |  |  |  |  |  |
|  |  |  |  |  |  |  |  | X |  |  |  |  |  |  |  |
|  | X |  |  |  |  |  |  |  |  |  |  |  |  | X |  |
|  |  |  |  | X |  |  |  |  |  |  |  |  |  |  |  |
|  |  |  |  |  |  |  |  |  |  |  |  |  |  |  |  |
|  |  |  |  |  |  |  |  |  |  |  |  |  |  |  |  |
| X |  |  |  |  |  |  |  |  |  |  |  |  |  |  | X |
|  |  |  |  |  |  |  |  |  |  |  |  | X |  |  |  |
|  |  |  |  |  |  |  |  |  |  |  |  |  |  |  |  |
|  |  |  |  |  |  |  |  |  |  |  |  | X |  |  |  |
|  |  |  |  |  |  | X |  |  | X |  |  |  |  |  |  |
|  |  |  |  |  |  |  |  |  |  |  |  |  |  | X |  |
|  |  |  |  |  | X |  |  |  |  |  |  |  |  | X |  |
|  |  |  | X |  |  |  |  |  |  |  |  |  |  |  |  |
| X | X |  |  |  |  | X |  | X |  |  | X |  |  | X | X |
|  |  |  |  |  |  |  | X |  |  | X |  |  |  |  |  |
|  |  | X |  |  |  |  |  |  |  |  |  |  |  |  |  |
|  |  |  |  |  | X |  |  |  |  |  |  |  |  |  | X |
|  |  |  |  | X |  |  |  |  |  |  |  |  |  |  |  |
|  |  |  |  |  |  | X |  |  |  |  |  |  |  |  | X |
|  |  |  |  |  |  |  |  |  | X |  |  |  |  |  |  |
| X |  |  |  |  |  | X |  | X |  | X |  |  |  |  |  |

## Symptoms of Homeopathic Remedies Chart

| Check if YES | Symptoms | Argentum nit. | Arsenicum alb. | Baryta carb. | Belladonna | Calcarea carb. | Calcarea phos. | Carcinosium | Chamomilla |
|---|---|---|---|---|---|---|---|---|---|
| | Intense | | | | X | | | | |
| | Jealous | | | | | | | | |
| | Kind | | | | | | | | |
| | Lacks self confidence | | | | | | | | |
| | Likes putting things together | | | | | | | | |
| | Likes to sing and dance | | | | | | | | |
| | Loses things | | | | | | | | |
| | Loves science fiction | | | | | | | | |
| | Memory problems | | | | | | | | |
| | Messy | | | | | | | X | |
| | Methodical -one task at a time | | | | | X | | | |
| | Mischievious | | | | | X | | | |
| | Mistakes in speaking & writing | X | | | | | | | |
| | Mood swings | | | | | | | | |
| | Neat | | X | | | | | | |
| | Negative | X | | | | | | | |
| | Never enough time | | | | | | | | |
| | Nightmares | | | | X | X | | X | |
| | Obsessive-compulsive | | | | | | | | |
| | Obstinate | | | | | X | | X | |
| | Organized | | | | | | | | |
| | Perfectionist | | X | | | | | | |
| | Performance anxiety | | | | | | | | |
| | Picks nose | | | | | | | | |
| | Plays tricks | | | | | | X | | |
| | Poor learning ability | | | | X | | | | |

## Symptoms of Homeopathic Remedies Chart (page 3)

| Cina | Hyoscamus | Ignatia | Lachesis | Lycopodium | Medorrhinum | Natrum mur. | Nux vomica | Phosphorus | Platina | Pulsatilla | Stramonium | Sulfur | Tarantula hisp. | Tuberculinum | Veratrum alb. |
|---|---|---|---|---|---|---|---|---|---|---|---|---|---|---|---|
|  | X |  | X |  |  |  |  |  |  |  |  |  |  |  |  |
|  |  |  |  |  |  |  |  | X |  |  |  |  |  |  |  |
|  |  |  | X |  |  |  |  |  | X |  |  |  |  |  |  |
|  |  |  |  |  |  |  |  |  |  |  | X |  |  |  |  |
|  |  |  |  |  |  |  |  |  |  |  |  | X |  |  |  |
|  |  |  |  |  |  |  |  |  |  |  | X |  |  |  |  |
|  |  |  |  |  |  |  |  |  |  |  | X |  |  |  |  |
|  |  | X |  |  | X |  |  | X |  | X |  |  |  |  |  |
|  |  |  |  |  |  |  |  |  |  |  | X |  |  |  |  |
|  |  |  |  |  |  |  |  |  |  |  |  |  | X |  |  |
|  |  | X |  | X |  |  |  |  |  | X |  |  |  |  |  |
|  |  |  | X |  | X |  |  |  | X | X |  |  |  |  |  |
|  |  |  |  |  |  | X |  |  |  |  |  |  |  |  |  |
|  |  |  |  |  |  |  |  |  |  |  |  |  | X | X |  |
|  |  |  |  |  |  |  |  |  | X |  |  |  |  |  |  |
|  |  | X |  |  | X |  |  |  |  | X |  |  |  | X |  |
|  |  | X |  |  |  |  |  |  |  |  |  |  |  |  |  |
|  |  |  |  |  |  |  |  | X |  |  |  |  |  |  |  |
|  |  |  |  |  |  | X |  |  |  |  |  |  |  |  |  |
|  |  |  |  | X | X |  |  |  |  |  |  |  |  |  |  |
| X |  |  |  |  |  |  |  |  |  |  |  |  |  |  |  |
|  |  |  |  |  |  |  |  |  |  |  |  |  |  |  |  |

## Symptoms of Homeopathic Remedies Chart

| Check if YES / Symptoms | Argentum nit. | Arsenicum alb. | Baryta carb. | Belladonna | Calcarea carb. | Calcarea phos. | Carcinosium | Chamomilla |
|---|---|---|---|---|---|---|---|---|
| Racing mind | | | | | | | | |
| Rebellious | | | | | | | | |
| Restless | | X | | | | X | | X |
| Sad disposition | | | | | | | | |
| Sarcastic | | | | | | | | |
| Save and collect things | | | | | | | | |
| Screams | | | | | | | | X |
| Self antagonism | | | | | | | | |
| Self conscious | | | X | | | | | |
| Sensitive to noise | | | | X | | | | |
| Shy | | | X | | | X | | |
| Strong sense of duty | | | | | | | | |
| Strong-willed | | | | | X | | | |
| Stubborn | | | | | X | | | |
| Swears | X | | | | | | | |
| Sympathetic | | | | | | | | |
| Suspicious | | | | | | | | |
| Takes chances | | | | | | X | | |
| Talkative | | X | | | | | | |
| Timid | | | X | | | | X | |
| Unable to be satisfied | | | | | | | | X |
| Violent | | | | | | | | |
| Wants to be center of attention | | | | | | | | |
| Worries about family | | | | | | | X | |
| **Total Number of X's** | | | | | | | | |

## Symptoms of Homeopathic Remedies Chart (page 4)

| Cina | Hyoscamus | Ignatia | Lachesis | Lycopodium | Medorrhinum | Natrum mur. | Nux vomica | Phosphorus | Platina | Pulsatilla | Stramonium | Sulfur | Tarantula hisp. | Tuberculinum | Veratrum alb. |
|---|---|---|---|---|---|---|---|---|---|---|---|---|---|---|---|
|  |  |  |  |  |  | X |  |  |  |  |  |  |  |  |  |
|  |  |  |  |  |  |  |  |  | X |  |  |  |  |  |  |
|  |  |  | X |  |  |  |  |  | X |  | X |  | X |  | X |
|  |  | X |  |  |  |  |  |  |  |  |  |  |  |  |  |
|  |  |  | X |  |  |  |  |  |  |  |  |  |  |  |  |
|  |  |  |  |  |  |  |  |  |  |  |  | X |  |  |  |
|  | X |  |  |  |  |  |  |  |  |  |  |  |  |  |  |
|  |  |  |  |  |  |  |  |  |  |  |  |  |  |  | X |
|  |  |  |  |  |  |  |  |  |  |  |  |  |  |  |  |
|  |  | X |  |  |  |  |  | X |  |  |  |  | X |  |  |
|  |  |  |  |  | X |  |  |  |  |  |  |  |  |  |  |
|  |  |  |  |  | X |  |  |  |  |  |  |  |  |  |  |
|  |  |  |  |  |  |  | X |  |  |  |  |  |  |  |  |
|  |  |  |  |  |  |  |  |  |  |  |  |  |  |  |  |
|  | X |  |  |  |  |  |  |  |  |  |  |  |  | X | X |
|  |  |  |  |  |  |  |  | X |  |  |  |  |  |  |  |
|  | X |  |  |  |  |  |  |  |  |  |  |  |  |  |  |
|  |  |  |  |  |  |  |  |  |  |  |  |  |  |  |  |
|  | X |  | X |  |  |  | X |  |  |  | X |  |  |  |  |
|  |  | X |  |  |  | X |  |  |  |  |  |  |  |  |  |
| X |  |  |  |  |  |  |  |  |  | X |  |  |  |  |  |
|  |  |  | X |  |  |  |  |  | X |  | X |  |  |  |  |
|  | X |  |  |  |  |  |  | X |  |  |  |  |  |  |  |
|  |  |  |  |  |  |  |  |  | X |  |  |  |  |  |  |
|  |  |  |  |  |  |  |  |  |  |  |  |  |  |  |  |

# *Common Remedies for Attention Deficit Disorder*

### Homeopathic Remedies for ADD

The homeopathic remedies listed here are further explanations for the remedies on the chart, and are commonly used for symptoms of Attention Deficit Disorder. Just by reading the lists of symptoms under each remedy, you may think that you fit more than one remedy. It is best to check off the specific symptoms you have in each list and then you can add up the total of checked symptoms. Use this list to confirm the top two or three homeopathic remedies found from the preceding chart.

**Argentum nitricum** – Silver nitrate
The people who can benefit from Argentum nitricum have mental anxiety. It is indicated for people who can be cruel and malicious, especially after being abused as a child. They -
- o   are impulsive, always seem in a hurry to do something, but do not accomplish anything.
- o   walk fast or are in continual motion.
- o   do not like to be late, and hurry to finish tasks.
- o   do not want projects that they cannot finish, so they are not willing to try new things.
- o   will have physical symptoms that get worse when angered or excited.

o   can be melancholy, and have a fear that they will
     have an incurable disease.
o   will be more nervous at night.
o   can be apathetic, and there may be dullness in
     thinking because of the effort needed to think.
o   may have trouble finding the right word when
     speaking.
o   tend to crave sugar, but it causes diarrhea.
o   may have a conflicting mind, acting as if they
     lack a conscience.

**Arsenicum album** – Arsenic
Restlessness is one of the major characteristics of
Arsenicum album. Even though they look like they are
hyperactive, always on the go, they get exhausted from
the slightest exertion.  They
o   are very talkative.
o   are anxious and impulsive, always looking to
     change position.
o   can be irritable, or angry, with despair and
     hopelessness.
o   tend to fear death, fear of being left alone, with a
     tendency to be a hypochondriac, worried about
     their health and their future.
o   are very detail-orientated. They like everything
     to be in order. Their surroundings are neat and
     organized. They are obsessed with having their
     homes clean.
o   have very high standards for themselves and will
     set goals for themselves that are difficult to
     obtain.
o   will have more energy in the morning and less in
     the evening. Their symptoms are often worse
     around midnight.

- o may have eating disorders. They tend to be sensitive to various foods.
- o will sip their water, yet be very thirsty all the time.
- o will have chronic diarrhea when they eat the "wrong" foods. They will also tend toward digestive problems such as ulcers, indigestion, and irritable bowel syndrome.
- o also tend to have respiratory symptoms such as hay fever, allergies, a constant runny nose, and asthma.

**Baryta carbonica** - Barium carbonate
These people are slow to develop physically, mentally, and emotionally. Children have an aversion to play. There is a weakness of memory, with major learning difficulties. They

- o lack self-confidence, act timid, or act out like a class clown to compensate.
- o mistrust others. They have a lot of general fears and act cowardly and immature.
- o do not like to be criticized and have fears of making a mistake.

**Belladonna** – Deadly Nightshade plant
Belladonna is a poisonous herb that when potentized into homeopathic remedy is very safe. These people

- o have nervous anxiety with restlessness
- o are oversensitive of every sense.
- o tend to be forgetful, slow, and have a poor learning ability.
- o are easily frightened, discouraged, and agitated.
- o have nightmares and are especially afraid of ghosts.
- o look wild when angry.

o have large heads, with bright red cheeks.
o tend to be susceptible to ear infections, bright red sore throats, throbbing headaches, and spike high fevers quickly when sick.
o often crave cold drinks.

**Calcarea carbonica** – Calcium carbonate
They are labeled as self-willed or stubborn, yet have many fears especially of robbers, dogs, heights, and airplanes. They
o are afraid of any situation with potential risk to physical safety. They are cautious and protective of themselves.
o are easily frightened or offended, tend to be sad.
o are calm, sensitive and lazy people often feeling sluggish.
o often have nightmares and will be afraid of the dark because of them.
o are methodical learners where they do best when only doing one thing at a time.
o will tend to make mistakes in speaking.
o do not like to do work and will be indifferent and apathetic in social situations.
o often have an underlying impatience, and tend to be obstinate and mischievous, with a pessimistic disposition.
o have large heads and they tend to get tired very easily
o have a hearty appetite that can lead to excessive weight gain.
o prefer cold drinks and like sweet foods, ice cream and eggs.
o tend to have a slow metabolism and digestive disorders.

**Calcarea phosphorica** – Calcium phosphate
These people
- feel frustrated or dissatisfied with life.
- are restless but shy and fearful, even though they will take chances.
- like change in their life, and get fussy easily.
- tend to have slow comprehension in learning situations.
- complain of growing pains, especially in the long bones.
- tend to have abdominal bloating and gas pains.

**Carcinosinum** - Cancer nosode
Frequently there is a family history of cancer for those who benefit from this remedy. They
- are hyperactive and obstinate, and tend to over-extend themselves.
- often suffer from insomnia.
- can be fearful, worried about others, yet seem disinterested and timid in social situations.
- are sensitive to reprimands and have gloomy disposition.
- can appear dull of mind, disinterested, and averse to conversation.
- can be very sympathetic to others.
- can be very tidy or very messy.

**Chamomilla** – Chamomile herb
As children, they cry a lot and want to be carried. They
- can become quarrelsome and mischievous.
- have to have a frantic type of mental excitement, with a tendency to get frightened easily.
- tend to be frustrated and restless, or contrary, not knowing what they want.

o   may be labeled as bad tempered, irritable, and
impatient.
o   do tend to be hypersensitive to pain and be
adverse to touch.
o   like attention and will calm down when they get
it.

## Cina - Wormseed

Children will tend to pick their nose, have itchy ears,
and will crave sweets. Children can be especially
contrary and disobedient with very difficult behavior.
Nothing satisfies them for long. They
o   are very hyperactive with a tendency to be
restless, fidgety and anxious.
o   are very curious about new things, but tend to be
disobedient and irritable in social situations.
o   do not like to be touched or even looked at.
o   have restless sleep, accompanied by jerking or
grinding of their teeth.
o   may have parasites such as pinworms causing
this restlessness.

## Hyoscyamus – Henbane herb

They are hyperactivity with anguish and fear especially
of dark, dogs, and water. They
o   are impulsive with episodes of mania that may
include screaming or hitting.
o   tend to be jealous and manipulative, with lying
and resorting to violence with rage.
o   have delusions of being poisoned or being
betrayed.
o   are talkative, and try to make jokes of serious
situations.
o   laugh at inappropriate times, act ridiculous to be
the center of attention.

- o love to run around naked, like to shock others, often using curse words at a young age.
- o overreact due to feelings of abandonment or jealousy.

**Ignatia** – Seed of St. Ignatius Bean
This remedy is helpful when a person has suffered from some sort of shock, such as the death of a loved one. Many are unable to cope with the stresses they feel and they may sometimes act out irrationally. They

- o tend to be depressed from a deeply bottled up suppressed grief.
- o worry a great deal, and this worry can lead them to become hysterical.
- o are bright, and very excitable, with very high-strung personalities.
- o are very sensitive to noise.
- o have a tendency to sigh often, which is a sign that it is difficult for them to express some of their emotions.

**Lachesis** – Venom of the bushmaster snake
They are restless and uneasy, and do not want to focus on business but wants to be somewhere else all the time. They

- o have anxiety, fears and discouragement that bring on tears and depressed thoughts.
- o express their emotions very easily.
- o are agitated about their situation, and will react in a nasty or sarcastic way.
- o tend to be insulting to others to cover up their own jealousy and lack of self-confidence.
- o are often very talkative.
- o do not like authority and tend to be difficult to live with since they are so suspicious of others.

**Lycopodium** – Club moss
They may seem to be irritable and obstinate, or overbearing. Yet they are really mild and submissive, with indifference to mental exertion.  They
- o   lack self-confidence but will be dictatorial at home where they feel safe.
- o   are cocky or act like bullies to cover up their own insecurities.
- o   fear looking bad, are afraid of failure, and do not like to try anything new.
- o   have performance anxiety, and have tendency to suffer from dyslexia, confusing words and letters.
- o   have trouble remembering what they read.
- o   crave chocolate and other sweets, and tend to have abdominal gas.
- o   get more tired, restless, and irritable between 4 and 8 p.m.

**Medorrhinum** – Gonorrhea virus nosode
They can have a Jekyll-Hyde personality where they switch from a manic personality to a mild personality quickly. They
- o   are irritable, hyperactive and always in a hurry.
- o   tend to have a racing mind with anxiety and delusions that something bad is going to happen.
- o   tend to be forgetful of names.
- o   time moves too slowly.
- o   tend to be obsessive-compulsive, and have trouble concentrating their thoughts and finding the right words.
- o   are apprehensive and impatient with feelings of insanity.
- o   have a fear of the dark, and a tendency to be suicidal.

**Natrum muriaticum** – Sodium chloride (table salt)
They tend to have high expectations of themselves and others. This causes internal anxiety, fear about the future, and hurriedness. When stressed about school or work they tend to get headaches and become forgetful. They

- o   hold their emotions inside, especially old disappointment and grief issues.
- o   take care of others, denying their own needs.
- o   prefer to be alone and do not like to be consoled when things go wrong.
- o   can be sad and indifferent, remembering the bad events in life. Yet there is an underlying impatience and irritability.
- o   tend to act timid in social situations.
- o   will get exhausted after talking or other mental exertion, and begin to make mistakes or become distracted.
- o   are extremely watchful, do not want to lose control in social situations.
- o   usually are sweet, except with their family.
- o   may display shyness with urination, especially in a public place.
- o   crave salty, starchy, and sour foods.

**Nux vomica** – Poison nut
They tend to have addictions to alcohol, cigarettes, or drugs to deal with their anxiety, restlessness, anger and irritability. They

- o   tend to be a hypochondriac, yet stubborn.
- o   finds fault and will carry grudges from past events.
- o   are uneasy about their health and are eager to speak about their disease.

o  have anxiety and agitation with palpations of the heart.
o  have deep inner fears that motivate them to action.
o  feel angry and frustrated, and they become sick when things don't work out according to their plans.
o  are sensitive to light and music, and do not like to be touched.
o  can be spiteful and malicious with a tendency to criticize.
o  are often constipated and have other digestive disturbances.
o  feel better after taking a short nap or sleeping.

**Phosphorus** - Phosphorus
They have an animated, imaginative, colorful personality always looking to charm everyone around them. They
o  like to be the center of attention, and have a fear of being unloved.
o  are good natured, sympathetic, and kind to others.
o  are often very artistic and creative.
o  can be spacy.
o  tend to act out to get attention, and will do what it takes to get it.
o  are often lively and passionate, but can also become forgetful or indifferent.
o  are very sensitive to electricity and thunderstorms, can sense a change of weather.
o  love to sleep for long hours.
o  tend to get upper respiratory diseases like bronchitis, pneumonia, colds, flu and asthma.

**Platina** – Platinum
They tend to find faults in others acting arrogant or aggressive in social situations. Yet, they lack self-confidence and have their own fears of rejection and failure. They
- o   have symptoms of insecurity, fear, and sadness.
- o   feel isolated and need to reconnect with the world.
- o   have a fear of death and often have sensations of dread.
- o   become distracted and forgetful, and they tend to live in and dwell on the past.

**Pulsatilla** – Windflower
This is a predominantly female remedy. They
- o   are very emotional, with mood swings, and changeable symptoms.
- o   easily cry and want to be nurtured. They like hugs.
- o   get upset easily and display their emotions freely.
- o   feel very vunerable, and are affected by hormonal shifts.
- o   feel better in fresh air and become worse in warm stuffy rooms.
- o   catch colds easily that last a long time.
- o   do not digest fatty foods well.

**Stramonium** – Jimsonweed
They are hyperactive people who tend to have violent tendencies. As children, they can be sweet all day and have terrors at night. There is mania or delusions with fixed ideas or great imagination. They
- o   tend to be inconsolable and irritated, with great activity and rapid movements.

- are self-willed and obstinate, and they have a desire to bite or hit others.
- are very talkative, speaking loudly and very fast
- have fears of the dark, of dogs, and of danger.
- tend to have hallucinations of terror.
- have constant nervousness and restlessness.
- have nightmares and may awake screaming having hallucinations of ghosts or imminent danger.
- can be very aggressive to others: hitting, biting, kicking, and using threatening language.

**Sulfur** – Sulfur mineral

They tend to be messy or untidy yet feel like they look fine. They

- are mechanically inclined, and like to take things apart and put them back to together.
- like to read and like computers.
- do not take care of themselves well.
- can be absent-minded and distracted easily.
- like to be constantly entertained.
- are forgetful, lose things, and have trouble remembering names.
- tend to be egotistical and are disposed to irritability and anger.
- can tend to be lazy when they need to do work.
- can be indecisive, tend to be awkward, have a weak memory, and weak social skills.
- like to collect things
- may have dry skin or other skin conditions like acne or eczema.
- have a need to scratch an itch, which can lead to restlessness.

o   are always feeling very hot, and at night they
     will throw off their covers because they get too
     warm.
o   feel weak at 11am, and will crave sweets to
     balance their blood sugar.


**Tarentula hispania** – Hispanic Tarantula
They are hyperactive, like to act wild and crazy, and feel
like there is never enough time. They
o   are mischievous and sneaky, and tend to tease
     others.
o   love to sing and dance to music, acting up more if
     not allowed to move.
o   are very restless and can have destructive
     impulses.


**Tuberculinum** - Tuberculosis nosode
They often feel dissatisfied about life, and may switch
between mania and depression. They
o   will rebel against restriction, and seek change
     and new experiences.
o   are irritable when waking up.
o   are afraid of dogs and other animals.
o   are compulsive and uncontrollable, leading to
     destructive tendencies.
o   will throw tantrums, become malicious, and
     break things.
o   have hallucinations that they can fly, or that
     someone is following them.

**Veratrum album** - Hellebore plant
They are often busy, but do not accomplish much. They
- are restless and hyperactive, and act on impulses.
- can be depressed or discouraged, and can become angry easily.
- are talkative with a tendency to swear.
- tend to find faults in others and will lie about themselves, trying to improve other people thoughts about them.
- have a racing mind and agitated actions; and have impulses to kiss or touch others.
- may be overly religious.

# *Using Homeopathic Remedies*

## Homeopathy – Potencies and Dosages

The numbers listed next to the names on homeopathic remedies can be confusing. These are the potency numbers. Commonly, the lowest potencies that are found in health food stores are 3X or 6X. These low potency remedies act faster and last for a shorter length of time, so they can be given every hour, and in some cases, every fifteen minutes. They are usually used in acute situations such as bee stings, muscle sprains or a sudden bout of diarrhea. Remedies with 30C potency are a medium high potency. They are given in cases where the symptoms have been around a longer time, such as a cold or digestive condition, and are usually taken one to three times per day. High potency remedies, such as 200C or 1M, are the strongest. They have longer lasting and more profound effects and are usually reserved for mental and emotional symptoms. For Attention Deficit Disorder symptoms, I recommend beginning with a 30C potency remedy, and moving up to a 200C only when necessary.

People who are beginners in using homeopathic remedies will primarily find the lower potencies in health food stores. These potencies are usually in the single digits such as the 6th potency (written as "6X" or "6C"), and are usually found in combination remedies that come in tablet form. Higher 30th potencies ("30X" or "30C") are found as classical remedies in health food stores in multi-dose tubes containing little round pellets. The 6X is a dose of the substance that has been diluted in 10 drops of water/alcohol mixture six times with vigorous shaking between each dilution, while the 6C remedy has been diluted in 100 drops of water/alcohol mixture six times. Only homeopathic practitioners who have more knowledge of homeopathy have access to the higher potencies (200C, 1M, or higher). It is important to remember that homeopathic remedies are more powerful the higher the potency number, and they have a deeper longer lasting action at these high potencies.

Homeopaths have found that people with acute injuries or ailments tend to need more frequent repetitions of low potency homeopathic doses shortly after injury. One may need to take a remedy every 30 to 60 minutes immediately after an injury. After a couple of hours, the frequency of doses can be reduced to every few hours, or 2 to 3 times per day depending upon the severity of pain. In homeopathy you only use the remedy until the pain or symptom subsides. It does not control symptoms, so when you choose the correct remedy the symptoms will not return once the remedy is stopped if it was the correct potency. Otherwise you may have to repeat it for another short period of time.

When using homeopathic remedies for Attention Deficit Disorder, I recommend using a 30C potency if you are self-prescribing. If you are working with a homeopathic practitioner you may be able to go up to a 200C, but only under their supervision. I hesitate to recommend how often to take the homeopathic remedy, because it depends on the severity of the symptoms. Usually, one dose of 3 pellets is recommended one to three times per day for no more than 1 week, and then re-evaluate the symptoms. Again, when symptoms begin to improve it is important to discontinue the remedy. If symptoms do not improve or improve a little, and you are sure you have the correct remedy, then you can increase the dosage for a few days. If after 3 days there is no improvement, then there is a good chance that the remedy will not make a difference. The actions of homeopathic remedies continue working for 20 to 30 days even after you stop taking it. So unless you anti-doted the remedy, it will keep on working.

**Directions for Taking Homeopathic Remedies**
Homeopathic remedies, whether they are in tablets, pellets, or in liquid form should not be taken with food. At least 15 minutes should separate the time between taking the remedy and eating or drinking anything except water. This includes toothpaste, cigarettes, and coffee. In fact, drinking coffee or smoking cigarettes should be at least 1 hour away from taking a remedy. So if you just took a remedy you will have to wait at least one hour before drinking coffee, or smoking. And if you just smoked or drank coffee, you should wait one hour before taking a remedy.

Also some substances can antidote, or neutralize, the effects of the homeopathic remedy. Common antidotes are coffee, mint, and other strong odors, like camphor. When you take one of these substances you can totally undo the good effects of homeopathic remedies. It is recommended to give a remedy at least 48 hours to begin to work before taking a substance that may antidote it. But it is more ideal to totally avoid any of the antidoting substances for about 30 days to give the remedy the time it may need to fully act.

When taking a homeopathic remedy, it is not recommended to touch the pellets, or put your lips on the dropper when it is a liquid remedy. Contaminating the substance with our "germs" can also antidote the action of the remedy. Keeping the container away from high temperatures, electric fields, and strong odors will also help maintain the potency of the remedy.

You can usually take a homeopathic remedy with other medications. They work on a different level, and do not counteract the action of medications. The way the medication controls the symptoms may make it difficult for you to notice if the homeopathic remedy is working. Yet, most often the change in behaviors can be seen even while taking other medications.

Homeopathic remedies are very useful in reducing the stresses that cause Attention Deficit Disorder symptoms, and can work quickly also. I remember one incident when I was taking a homeopathic class. A little boy was hitting his mother while she was trying to explain his symptoms to us. The homeopathic doctor decided on the best remedy according to his symptoms, and gave it to him right in front of the class. He immediately calmed down. Similar reactions can be seen in many hyperactive clients who successfully use homeopathy, as well as for many other symptoms of Attention Deficit Disorder.

# Section 4

# *Learning Patterns and Attention Deficit Disorder*

# *Learning Patterns and Attention Deficit Disorder*

## Quick Find Outline

# How Does My Mind Think?

To really learn is to create meaning to what we have learned. Real knowledge occurs when we use all of our senses to create a real picture that relates to our world. Two ways to express knowledge are tests and practical use. When we take tests, whether they are multiple choice, fill in the blank, or essay questions, we are given the opportunity to find out if we really understand the concept or knowledge that we have been taught. Especially with essay tests, we get to express our personal knowledge of the topic in our own words. Even though essay tests are usually the type we want to avoid, probably because we feel we do not know the subject, they are the most valuable in reinforcing the knowledge in our memory. Practical use of new material is also necessary. When we can verbally explain or show someone how to do something we just learned we will be able to remember it better later on.

Learning is not all in the head. Whenever movement can be a part of learning it will increase the memory of the learning. This is why it is important to use as many senses in learning as possible. Movements from touching, hearing, experiencing, writing and even talking help us remember better. To remember a thought, an action must be made to anchor it. Think about meeting someone and forgetting his or her name before the conversation is over. You heard their name but did not create an anchor to remember it. By creating your own physical association you will be able to remember it. You can say their name back to them, or remember their name by correlating it to a specific physical feature.

We will be able to remember new information when we learn to use physical movements to correlate this knowledge. Writing letters or numbers is one type of physical movement. So is talking. Talking about what we have learned is the reason we have classroom settings in school. If talking about new knowledge was not necessary, we could read a book and remember it only using visual senses, and we would not have to have class discussions. Talking about what we learn with others helps to integrate and solidify the knowledge. Acetylcholine is the neurotransmitter that is secreted between neurons during talking that helps our memory. Consistent release of acetylcholine increases the number of nervous system dendrites improving long-term memory function. So both children and older adults need to express their new knowledge to others so that they can keep their memory active. This is why they say, "use it or lose it." If we no longer use our brains, our neurotransmitters will not function and our brains, especially our memory, will suffer.

Other movements besides talking can be used to remember also. Any repetitive movement can improve brain function. Some of our best ideas can come when we are walking, swimming, doing dishes, knitting, or even eating. Some people snack during learning sessions. This is a movement that helps to keep the brain functioning, even though in the long run excess pounds could be another problem.

Keeping an organized environment and time will help us learn also. Routine is important for most people with Attention Deficit Disorder. When adults and children have a set schedule, and repeat it enough times that it becomes a habit, remembering can come easier. Scattered times during the day for homework or exercise can lead to forgetting or putting it off until later. Having an organized workspace, or home environment, is also helpful in reducing stress on a daily basis. When we can find things when we need them, we will be less frustrated. Consistency of rules and schedules help all of us learn better by helping our brain focus more easily.

## Learning Patterns

There are assessment tests you can take to help you determine if you use your right brain or left brain more easily. Actually, all of us use both sides of our brain to learn. Yet, how we learn can be affected by whether we are more creative or analytical, which influences how we perceive the world around us.

Earlier we discussed about classifying people as right-brained or left-brained. Here we will look more specifically to the meaning of using your dominant left or right senses in learning. For example, very few people can write with both hands, so we are known as either right-handed or left-handed. Also when you use a phone, which ear do you use? Is it always the same ear, or do you switch ears depending on the phone situation? When we combine the way the brain works with the dominant body style we can discover potential thinking patterns that affect learning, concentration, and decision-making ability.

Our brain contains two hemispheres that are connected through the corpus callosum. This corpus callosum is the communication system between the right and left hemispheres of the brain. The left side of the brain controls the right side of the body, and the right side of the brain controls the left side of the body. So if you talk on the phone with your left ear, you are sending the main message to the right hemisphere of your brain. Also when you use your right hand to touch and feel any sensation you are sending the message first to your left hemisphere of your brain.

One creative **test for right or left brain dominance** is the chart on the back cover of this book. There is a list of common colors that are printed in different colors than the name of the color. For example, the first word is "lavender", but it is printed in a green colored font. The next word is "red", but is printed in a blue color. The idea of this left / right brain dominance test is to figure out if you can say the color of the word across and down instead of reading the word in a quick progression. If your right brain is functioning well you will be able to say each color of the word, instead of reading the words. When your left-brain is dominant, you will quickly jump from saying the colors to reading the words. See how far you get down the list of colors before your left brain jumps to reading the words. The farther down the list you go before switching to read the words indicates the dominance level of your right brain hemisphere. If you only get two lines down and you are already reading the words, then you are left brain dominant.

Each hemisphere processes additional types of information in a different manner. The left side of the brain is thought to be the more logical, detail-oriented side, and the right side of the brain is the more artistic, whole-picture side. In a few cases, these "sides" are transposed, so that the right side is more logical and the left side more artistic, but this is rare.

Some of the common traits of the left and right brain hemisphere are listed here:

| **Left Hemisphere** | **Right Hemisphere** |
|---|---|
| **Logical** | **Artistic** |
| Detailed oriented | Whole picture oriented |
| Looks at differences | Looks at similarities |
| Linear thinking | Intuition thinking |
| Thinks in sequences | Thinks all at once |
| Language focus | Feelings focus |
| Future thinking | "Now" thinking |
| Watches technique | Watches flow or movement |
| Controls own feelings | Free with feelings |
| Follow rules | Follow image |
| Plans events | Spontaneous with events |

We have both sides of the brain working all the time. Yet, when you check off your specific features you will commonly find one column may have many more checks than the other. If you do have a similar amount of checks on both sides, it indicates that your left and right hemispheres of your brain are working well together. If you are definitely more left or right brain dominant then you will benefit from some of the brain exercises that follow.

In the first section we talked about visual learners, vs. auditory learners, vs. kinesthetic learners. We all use our eyes, ears, and hands to learn, but we have a dominant way of learning, especially when we are under a lot of stress. When we have to learn something quickly, or when we give others directions, we give tend to use our dominant style of learning.

There are additional **tests** to see if your **visual, auditory, and kinesthetic learning** are affected by your brain dominance. These are simple tests to determine your dominant hand, foot, eye, and ear. We instinctively have a favorite hand to write with, which is pretty easy to determine. To determine which foot, ear, and eye you use predominantly, you will need to find a piece of three-ring binder paper, or paper with holes punched in it to use for the following tests.

It is beneficial to do this procedure with someone else, called the "Tester," directing the person being tested, called the "Testee." Do these tests in a quick sequence so that the Testee does not get too long to think about what they "should" do, but what comes instinctively.

1. The Tester should give the paper to the Testee, either by putting it on a table, or handing it to them towards the centerline of their body. The Testee will pick it up, or grab it, with their dominant hand.

2. Then ask the Testee to "listen to the paper", or put it up to their ear, and notice which ear they cover. This is their dominant ear, or the ear they probably use to talk on the phone. You could also confirm this later by asking them which ear they most commonly use when talking on the phone.

3. Then have the Testee look through the hole in the paper at you. Notice which eye they use to look through the hole. This is their dominant eye.

4. Then crumble up the piece of paper and make it into a ball. Place it on the floor out in front of the centerline of their body, and have them kick the ball. See which foot they use to kick the ball. This is their dominant foot.

The Tester should write down each of the answers, and notice if there is a pattern to them. If is determined that the Testee is right or left brain dominant, and they have certain patterns to their eye, ear, hand and foot dominance, then specific recommendations can be made to improve their learning environment.

If the results show that the tested person uses their right hand, ear, eye, and foot, and is left-brain dominant, they can learn in a regular school situation more easily. Their physical information is going to the brain hemisphere that is dominant. The same thing is true when someone is left handed, and use their left ear, eye, and foot, to access information that is sent to their right-brain dominant hemisphere. Where it gets interesting is when there are different hand, feet, eye, and ear dominance. The following chart lists some of the patterns:

| Dominant Brain | Sense | Preferred Learning Style |
| --- | --- | --- |
| Left brain | Right hand | Verbal learner |
| Left brain | Left hand | Limited kinesthetic learning |
| | | |
| Left brain | Right eye | Visual learner |
| Left brain | Left eye | Limited visual learning |
| | | |
| Left brain | Right ear | Auditory learner |
| Left brain | Left ear | Limited auditory learner |
| | | |
| Right brain | Right hand | Limited communication |
| Right brain | Left hand | Kinesthetic learner |
| | | |
| Right brain | Right eye | Limited visual learning |
| Right brain | Left eye | Visual learner |
| | | |
| Right brain | Right ear | Limited auditory learner |
| Right brain | Left ear | Auditory learner |

Use this chart by circling your left or right brain dominance in the left column. Then circle your dominant senses in the middle column. You can then detect from this chart your preferred learning styles.

You can discern from this chart that having a left brain dominant hemisphere, along with a left hand, eye and ear dominance, the learning ability will be restricted. This type of person will have limited visual, auditory, and kinesthetic learning. This when it is most important to get the communication between the two brain hemispheres communicating more effectively. The same idea is true with right-handed people, who also are right ear and eye dominant, and then are also right brain dominant. The foot dominance is not as important as the other eye, ear, and hand dominance. It is used just to verify, in cases like the two extremes just explained, if the whole body is truly right dominated or left dominated.

Schools often teach students their lessons in more logical and sequential terms. The favorite mode of teaching is a step-by-step fashion, often leaving out what the meaning or value of the lesson, or how they will use this information in real life. Left hemisphere dominant people can more easily learn this way. Right hemisphere dominant people need to know how and when they will use the information, before they decide to put the effort out to learn it.

In cases where the student is left brained and left handed, but mainly uses their right ear, or right eye, they will need to understand that they are better visual or auditory learners, than verbal learners. They will not benefit from taking notes. It would be best for them to listen to the speaker, or see pictures that relate to the topic to remember the concept being learned.

Students who are left-handed are often right brain dominant. They are kinesthetic learners who like a "hands-on" approach. They need to take notes or do something with their hands to facilitate remembering the topic. Students who are left eye dominant and right brain dominant will be very interested in art and visual effects in movies. Those who are left ear dominant and right brain dominant will more likely have musical ability, or an interest in sound production. By noticing potentially dominant learning styles, you can help yourself or others improve the way they understand information, and actually reduce the stress of trying to learn like everyone else.

Improving the communication between the brain hemispheres is also important whenever there is excessive brain dominance or sensory dominance. In the following section we will look at specific brain exercises that help to improve communication in the corpus callosum between the two brain hemispheres, and other exercises to improve visual and auditory learning. These brain exercises also help to reduce nervous system stress and improve circulation throughout other parts of the body.

# *Stress Reduction and Mental Clarity Exercises*

### Brain Exercises

Meet "**Happy Harry.**" He is going to be our demonstrator for some simple exercises that can help to improve your brain and nervous system function.

Every learning situation has the same essential steps: sensory input, integration, assimilation and action. We need to realize with one of our senses that there is a message. Then we have to understand the message. At that point we can decide what to do about the message, and then act on it as we know or have been trained to do. Sometimes we do not receive these input messages to our brain as effectively as we should. This can cause us not to react as expected in school or work situations.

Brain exercises wake up the body/mind system, and help to improve the learning process. All types of exercise improve the structural system and improve the circulation of the blood to the brain. Yet these specific brain exercises also help to enhance mental performance.

Many teachers use these brain exercises to facilitate learning in their students. These simple movement exercises can help at school or work to keep oxygen flowing to the brain, lymph, and nervous system. When we sit still too long we will tend to either fall asleep or begin to lose focus. These specific movements will get more oxygen to our brain that can help enhance sensory input. We will look at a few movement exercises that improve brain circulation making it easier to understand what you read and hear by balancing both sides of the brain and increasing brain communication between the left and right hemispheres. Paul Dennison, Ph.D. in the 1970's, researched many movements and exercises that affect learning. He developed a program called Educational Kinesiology to work with people who were learning disabled. His exercises are called Brain Gym movements. I will be showing you my favorite movements that I use to evaluate brain communication, and enhance learning.

### Left/Right Brain Communication

How do you know if your left and right brain are communicating well? Copy Happy Harry by putting both of your palms out to your side. Bring your palms together in front of your body, and clasp your hands together. Did your hands go together easily? Or did they not quite meet in the  middle. People who are having trouble thinking clearly, for example, people who are drunk, will have trouble doing this exercise successfully. When someone is excessively stressed they will have trouble doing this exercise also. The fingers may not come together easily, or you may have to think about the motion to make it work. The fingers should smoothly move into place. This is an introductory exercise to help you determine how your left and right brain are communicating. If you are having difficulty doing this exercise, do the following brain exercises and then try this movement again and see if it is easier.

For people with difficulty thinking clearly there are certain movements that help to bring the brain and senses into better focus. The five exercises I teach to children and adults with attention problems are explained below. They are:

### Cross Patterning

In aerobic exercise class there is a common movement that involves lifting one knee and touching it with the opposite hand or elbow. Then this movement continues by putting the bent leg back on the ground and lifting the other knee and touching it with the other hand or elbow. By doing this movement of one hand touching the opposite raised knee continually for 30 to 60 seconds you actually are improving the nervous system communication between both of your brain hemispheres.

Cross patterning is a cross lateral pattern of walking in place that activates large areas of both the right and left brain hemispheres to improve communication that in turn creates a higher level of reasoning. This exercise can be done slowly to improve motor skills and balance, and improve decision-making ability that is activated in the frontal lobe of the brain in the forehead area. I often have children try to do this Cross Patterning movement in my office while I demonstrate it to them. The children who have trouble reading often have the most difficulty with this movement. I often ask if they crawled as a baby. Crawling helps to coordinate left and right movements and takes both halves of the brain working together to accomplish it. I recommend this exercise to anyone who is having trouble putting together thoughts in their mind or on paper. If a child or adult cannot do this movement I have them practice very slowly until they are able to do it easily. It is a very important tool in improving brain communication. Jumping rope is another similar exercise. I know of children who practice skipping rope, switching legs while jumping, while twirling their own rope to greatly improve mental ability. Any similar exercise using opposite hands and feet in movements will help, such as free-style swimming, skiing, and many exercise machines that use both arms and legs in opposing movements.

### Sideways 8's

Another exercise that helps to get the right and left brain communicating is a simple hand movement called Sideways 8's. In this movement you grasp both of your hands together in front of you and put both thumbs straight up so that they are in your main field of vision. While keeping your head straight forward, hold your arms out in front of you. Imagine a lazy 8 or the number

8 on its side, and trace it with your hands while watching your thumbs. Begin by bringing both hands up in the center and traveling in a circular pattern up and over to the right, then coming back down around to the left, and coming back up in the center of your body. Then go around again in the center toward the left side making another circle. Continue this motion making circles on both the right and left sides always going up in the middle of your body. Do this pattern continuously for 30 seconds while watching your thumbs with your eyes, without moving your head. By doing this pattern with your hands together you are activating both sides of your brain to work in cooperation. This sideways 8 pattern helps to get both sides of your brain coordinated so that you can focus on a task or assignment.

This exercise can be done writing on paper using one hand at a time and then using both hands. Five or more continuous sideways 8's patterns help bring the brain into focus. When they are written it helps to improve visual tracking and hand/eye coordination. This exercise helps to relieve writer's block and improves test-taking ability. When done in the air it helps improve eye muscle coordination and fine motor tracking. It is good exercise to use to reduce eyestrain after working at a computer.

Elementary school teachers use these two exercises to focus attention in the classroom after lunch or any disruption in their schedule. These two movements – the Cross Patterning and Sideways 8's are even useful to do before a new subject is going to be learned and the teacher wants the students to be paying close attention. By doing these exercises regularly, both hemispheres of your brain will be able to focus better with visual, auditory, or kinesthetic learning patterns.

## Emotional Stress Releasing Points

There are three other movements I use to reduce stress and improve thinking ability. The first is called Emotional Stress Releasing Points. There are two neurovascular points on your forehead that are used to help you focus. These points are about one to two inches from the center and in the middle between the hairline and the eyebrows. These emotional stress-relieving points are real neurovascular points that affect your nervous and circulatory system.

You do not need to know exactly where these points are since you just need to lightly cover your forehead with your hand to activate the points. Have you ever seen someone under stress, or when taking a test, cover their forehead with their hand? This is an instinctive movement that we use when we are under stress and we want our brain to focus better so that the stress is reduced.

This movement is something you can do to yourself easily, or you can hold your hand lightly over another person's forehead and tell them to breathe. They will begin to feel more relaxed if they were already stressed. I have used this movement with others often when they do not know what they want, or they have had a trauma and they have lots of anxiety. I encourage children to do this when they are taking a test, so that they can focus better and make good decisions on the correct answer.

## Eye Rotations

Eye rotation exercises help you learn better visually. If you have trouble seeing everything that is happening during a movie, or do not remember what you see very well, you will benefit from eye movement exercises. Begin eye rotations by holding one arm out in front of you with two fingers pointing out. Make large circles in your field of vision clockwise five times, and then switch to counterclockwise five times. While you are making these circles, watch your pointing fingers. Keep your head straight and not moving, and rotate your eyes to watch the circles.

Make large circles to stretch your visual field. Notice if you have trouble seeing your fingers in all areas of your vision. If you begin blinking or stop looking at your fingers, this may be a stressed area of your visual field. Do additional circles until this visual area is watched easily, without blinking. By rotating your eyes beyond your normal visual field, you will be able to expand your visual distance, and see and experience more in your daily life. This helps you live life without "blinders on."

If you work at a computer all day long, or have eye strain from reading or paperwork, you can relieve the strain by touching points on the back of your skull. These eye points on the back of your head are often sore when you have eyestrain. These points are located on the lower part of your skull in an indentation about one to two inches from the spinal column. I rub these points before and after I do any eye movement exercises.

## Ear Pulls

To increase awareness, to improve energy and to improve circulation to the whole body, I use ear pulls. Our ears have over 400 acupuncture points that can be used to improve many health related issues. One way you can stimulate your whole body is to pull on your ears in all directions. Pull them up, out, down, try to unroll the edges. The more you can move the cartilage in the ear, the added stimulation you will get to these acupuncture points. I have used ear pulls to stay awake in class, while driving (only one hand  pulling on one ear at time), and to reduce neck tension and stiffness. This exercise improves circulation throughout your whole body, and can help improve your listening skills.

In the first section we talked about how stress affects our lives, and how movements or exercise can reduce stress. These movements are specific stress releases for specific areas of our brain and nervous system. They may seem too simple to be effective, but just do them when you get stressed. First, see if you can do the Left/Right Brain Integration exercise. If that seems easy, touch your eye points on the back of your head and see if they are sore. Even if they are not sore, it is good to rub these points regularly to prevent eyestrain.

If you are having trouble focusing on your work do some Cross Patterning exercises and Sideway 8's circles.

Then go back to your work and see if it is easier. If you have to make some decisions and cannot think clearly, do Emotional Stress Releasing Points and breathe, and see how it helps you focus your thoughts. These exercises do help many people, and can make a large difference in children who are having trouble learning.

# Putting It All Together

*"Every child has inside him an aching void for excitement, and if we don't fill it with something which is exciting and interesting and good for him, he will fill it with something which is exciting and interesting and which isn't good for him."*

- Theodore Roosevelt

We have looked at a variety of different topics that can be used to help understand ourselves, or our children, with Attention Deficit Disorder symptoms, as well as those who are just having trouble thinking more clearly. Where do you first begin to make a difference? Do you understand your symptoms better now? Have you seen what may be causing them to occur? Is some stress pattern or nutritional deficiency creating them?

The information in the first section on the neurotransmitters and their relationship to Attention Deficit Disorder was included to show that neurological problems can come from daily stress and nutritional imbalances. Changing specific neurotransmitter deficiencies may seem difficult, because they vary so much with dietary food choices and supplementation.

So, first I recommend focusing on the quality of foods in your daily diet to make the difference in your thinking ability and behavior difficulties. If you are working with children, make sure they get rid of all food colorings in their foods, and get whole foods in their diet, not processed foods with fillers and preservatives. It disturbs me when parents say it is too difficult to change their child's diet. The children are not the ones doing the grocery shopping, so the parents can buy natural foods instead of highly processed foods. Buy whole fruits and vegetables instead of Fruit Roll-ups, even canned fruits without heavy syrup is better than these fake fruits. Buy cereal without colorings, and lower amounts of sugar. The less boxed foods they eat the healthier they will be.

Children can and will change to eat what they have available at home when they get hungry. Buy real brick cheese instead of colored cheese foods already wrapped in slices. All of these processed foods have more preservatives, colorings, and food additives so that they can stay on the shelf longer. Do you know a Twinkie will never rot away? That is because it has no nutrition that is found in real foods. Real fruits and vegetables will get moldy because the enzymes and minerals interact to break down the food when it is exposed to oxygen. Your body will not break down the Twinkie either and it will cause stress on your digestive system.

Do not buy any foods with partially hydrogenated fats or high fructose corn syrup. Just by avoiding these additives you will automatically have to buy healthier foods. These trans fat and highly processed sugar products are the two main culprits affecting cholesterol levels, triglyceride levels, blood sugar levels, causing many chronic health problems including allergies.

For adults, I would make sure you are getting high quality nutrition and nutritional supplements on a daily basis. Get a balance of nutrients including antioxidants to reduce free radicals, minerals and enzymes for energy, and B-complex vitamins for your nervous system stress. Add essential fatty acids to balance your blood sugar, reduce inflammation, and improve metabolism.

Do not take separate amino acids to balance neurotransmitters without first changing your diet and nutritional supplements. When taking amino acids, it is not recommended to take them with protein foods, or their benefit will be diminished. It is best to take specific amino acids with carbohydrate foods, or on an empty stomach to get their full action. Yet, keeping neurotransmitters in balance is achieved easily by maintaining a good balance of nutrients, including sufficient protein levels, in your digestive system.

Children need good nutritional supplements also, but not in overdose amounts. A complete complement of antioxidants, B-complex vitamins, and minerals are important for them too. If you are not taking a whole food supplement, look in the Resources section for more information available on Juice Plus+® and the Children's Research Study.

The Homeopathic Symptoms Chart can help you understand your personality and symptoms better. This is a good checklist for you to use for yourself, and have other family members complete with their opinion of your personality. Sometimes other people's opinions can help you understand what personality you are showing to the world, and help you find a constitutional homeopathic remedy that fits your personality profile. By using the correct homeopathic remedy you will reduce layers of stress that will help you or your child cope with the pressures of life and learning. Stress is a factor in all of our lives. We cannot always get rid of it easily. But we can make our response to it different. When we can reduce anxiety and tension using homeopathic remedies and nutrition, stress will not accumulate and we will prevent chronic disease conditions better.

Understand your own learning process. If your brain is balanced you will automatically think better. When you get stressed you will fall into your specific learning pattern and you may have to compensate until the stress is relieved. But now you know some brain exercises that will improve communication between your brain hemispheres. You can improve your visual and auditory learning, and do Emotional Stress Releasing Points to make decision-making easier.

Attention Deficit Disorder does not have to stop you or your child from experiencing life. You do not have to use medications to control your symptoms. You can make a difference in behavior by understanding where the stress is coming from and dealing with it. You now have many natural choices for Attention Deficit Disorder to use and share with others.

# Resources

## Attention Deficit Disorder Online Resources

**ADD Resources** – Non-Profit Corporation
http://www.addresources.org/
Attention Deficit Disorder Resources helps people with
ADD or ADHD achieve their full potential.

**Children and Adults with Attention-
Deficit/Hyperactivity Disorder (CHADD)** is a
national non-profit organization founded in 1987 in
response to the frustration and sense of isolation
experienced by parents and their children with AD/HD.
http://www.chadd.org/

## Other Resources

**Children's Research Project**
For more information on the children' s whole food
nutrition project contact: www.ChildrensResearch.org
or www.askdrsears.com
For information on Juice Plus whole food nutrition,
go to: www.JuicePlus.com

**Brain Gym® International**
1575 Spinnaker Drive, Suite 204B
Ventura, CA 93001
edukfd@earthlink.net
phone: (800) 356-2109 or (805) 658-7942

**Feingold Assn. of the U.S.**
Suite 106, 127 East Main St.
Riverhead, NY 11901
631-369-9340
fausmem@aol.com
http://www.feingold.org
Help for families of children with learning or behavior
problems, including attention deficit disorder. Supports
members in implementing the Feingold program.
Generates public awareness on the role of food, diet and
synthetic additives.

**Kiersey Temperament Test**
http://www.advisorteam.com/temperament_sorter/about/
Temperament is a set of inclinations that each of us is
born with; it's a predisposition to certain attitudes and
actions.

**Learning Strategies Corporation**
2000 Plymouth Road
Minnetonka, Minnesota 55305-2335
Toll-Free 800-735-8273
http://www.learningstrategies.com/
Maximize your potential with books, tapes and training
from Learning Strategies Corporation.

**Glycemic Index / Glycemic Load Report**
Natural Choices, Inc.
www.NaturalChoicesForYou.com
Newsletters and information directed toward preventing
diabetes and improving health naturally. A report called
*"Yes, You Can Have Carbohydrates!"* is available online.

# Bibliography

Anastopoulos, Arthur D.; Klinger, Erika E.; Temple, E. Paige. "Treating children and adolescents with attention-deficit/hyperactivity disorder." Handbook of psychological services for children and adolescents., Oxford University Press: New York, NY, US, 2001. p. 245-266.

Armstrong, Thomas, Ph.D., *The Myth of the ADD Child* (New York: Dutton, 1995).

Barbaresi, W., *Approach to the Diagnosis and Management of Attention-Deficit Hyperactivity Disorder*. Mayo Clinic Proc 1996: 71; 463-471

Barkley RA: Attention-deficit Hyperactivity Disorder: A Handbook for Diagnosis and Treatment. New York, NY: Guilford Press; 1990.

Barkley RA. *Taking Charge of ADHD*. New York: The Guilford Press, 2000, p. 21.

Bornstein, R et al, *Plazma Amino Acids in Attention Deficit Disorder* Psychiatry Research 1990 33(3) 301-306

Braverman Eric R., M.D., *The Healing Nutrients Within,* Basic Health Publications; 2003

Carlson CL, Pelham WE Jr, Milich R, Dixon J, *Single and Combined Effects of Methylphenidate and Behavior Therapy on the Classroom Performance of Children with Attention-Deficit Hyperactivity Disorder*. J Abnormal Child Psychol 1992: 20 (2); 213-232

Carter CM, Urbanowicz M, Hemsley R, et al. Effects of a few food diet in attention deficit disorder. Arch Dis Child 1993;69:564–8.

Eli Lilly and Company, Indianapolis, IN, December 17, 2004 - announced today it has added a warning to the label for Strattera, an attention deficit/ hyperactivity disorder medication. http://www.add.org/news/strattera_label.html

Elia J, Ambrosini PJ, Rapoport JL: Treatment of attention-deficit-hyperactivity disorder. *New England Journal of Med.*, 1999 Mar 11; 340(10): 780-8

Goldman LS, Genel M, Bezman RJ, Slanetz PJ: Diagnosis and treatment of attention-deficit/hyperactivity disorder in children and adolescents. *Council on Scientific Affairs, American Medical Association.* JAMA 1998 Apr 8; 279(14): 1100-7

Greenhill, Laurence L., Mary V. Solanto, Ed; Amy Frances Torrance Arnsten, "Clinical effects of stimulant medication in ADHD." Stimulant drugs and ADHD: *Basic and Clinical Neuroscience.* Oxford University Press: New York, NY, US, 2001. p. 31-71

Johnson T, "Evaluating the hyperactive child in your office: Is it ADHD?" American Family Physician 1997 Jul; 56(1): 155-60, 168-70

*Journal of Pediatrics,* February 1996 cited in *Well Being Journal,* May/June 1996.

Mandel, Boris M., FS. Foods and additives are common causes of the attention deficit hyperactive disorder in children. Ann Allergy 1994;72: 462–8.

Mendelsohn M.D., Robert S. *How to Raise a Healthy Child...In Spite of Your Doctor* (New York: Ballantine Books, 1984)

Murphy K, Barkley, RA. *Journal of Attention Deficit Disorder,.* Experts estimate 4 percent of adults in the United States, more than 8 million people, have ADHD. 1996; 1:147-161.

Murray, N.D., Michael and Pizzorno, N.D., Joseph *An Encyclopedia of Natural Medicine* (Rocklin, California: Prima Publishing, 1990)

Nahlik JE, Searight HR: Diagnosis and treatment of attention deficit hyperactivity disorder. Primary Care Report 1996; 2: 65-74.

Nemzer, E et al, *Amino Acid Supplementation as Therapy for Attention Deficit Disorder* Journal of American Academy of Child and Adolescent Psychiatry, 1986 25(4) 509-513

*Newsweek* "Does My Child Need Ritalin? Stimulants are still the most effective treatment for ADHD. The challenge is to use them wisely." (2000). April, 135(17): p81.

*Practice Parameters for the Assessment and Treatment of Children, Adolescents and Adults With Attention Deficit/Hyperactivity Disorder,* Journal of American Academy of Child and Adolescent Psychiatry, 36:10 Supplement, October 1997

Prinz RJ, Roberts WA, Hantman E., Dietary correlates of hyperactive behavior in children. J Consult Clin Psychol 1980;48:760–9.

Reichenberg-Ullman N.D., M.S.W., Judyth "Homeopathy for Hyperactive Children," in *Natural Health*, Nov/Dec 1992

Ricco C.A. *et al.,* "Neurological Basis of Attention Deficit Hyperactivity Disorder," *Exceptional Children, 60* (1993): 118-124.

Rosen LA, Booth SR, Bender ME, et al. Effects of sugar (sucrose) on children's behavior. J Consult Clin Psychol 1988;56:583–9.

Rowe KS, Rowe KJ. Synthetic food coloring and behavior: a dose response effect in a double-blind, placebo-controlled, repeated-measures study. J Pediatr 1994;125:691–8.

Shaywitz, S & Shaywitz, B *Biologic Influences in Attentional Deficit Disorders* in Levine, M et al, Developmental-Behavioral Pediatrics, W.B. Saunders Company, Philidelphia 1983

Smith, M.D., Lendon *Feed Your Kids Right* (New York: Dell Publishing, 1979)

Strohecker, James, editor. *Alternative Medicine: The Definitive Guide* (Puyallup, Washington: Future Medicine Publishing, 1994)

Taylor, M *Evaluation and Management of Attention-Deficit Hyperactivity Disorder.* American Family Physician 1997: 55 (3); 887-894

Thurston, LP *Comparison of the Effects of Parent Training and of Ritalin in Treating Hyperactive Children* In: Strategic Interventions for Hyperactive Children Gittlemen M, ed New York: ME Sharpe, 1985 pp 178-185

Ullman N.D., Robert & Reichenberg-Ullman N.D., M.S.W., Judyth, *Ritalin-Free Kids* (Rocklin, California: Prima Publishing, 1996)

Wender PH: Pharmacotherapy of attention-deficit/hyperactivity disorder in adults. J Clin Psychiatry 1998; 59 Suppl 7: 76-9

Whitaker, Julian *Dr. Whitaker's Guide to Natural Healing* (Rocklin, CA: Prima Publishing, 1996)

Wilens TE: Straight Talk about Psychiatric Medications for Kids. New York, NY: Guilford Press; 1999.

Wolraich ML, ed: The Classification of Child and Adolescent Mental Diagnoses in Primary Care: Diagnostic and Statistical Manual for Primary Care (DSM-PC) Child . Elk Grove, Ill: American Academy of Pediatrics; 1996

Wolraich ML, Wilson DB, White JW, The effect of sugar on behavior or cognition in children. A meta-analysis. JAMA 1995; 274: 1617–21.

Wonder, E.H., "The Food Additive-Free Diet in the Treatment of Behavior Disorders: A Review," *Developmental and Behavioral Pediatrics 7 (1986): 35-42*

Zimmerman, C.N., Marcia *The ADD Nutrition Solution* (Owl Books, 1999)

# Index

## T

Tarentula hispania, 134
Temper tantrums, 14
Temperament, 23, 24,
    168
Thunderstorms, 131
Timid, 124, 126, 130
Trans fats, 91, 92, 95
Tyrosine, 36, 37, 85

## U

Under-methylated, 77

## V

Veratrum album, 102,
    135
Violent, 15, 18, 26, 132
Visual, 20, 21, 34, 146,
    149-153, 158, 160, 165
Vitamin A, 81
Vitamin B-3, 80, 87
Vitamin B-5, 81
Vitamin B-6, 80
Vitamin B-12, 77, 80, 92
Vitamin C, 4, 36, 37, 81,
    82, 85, 87, 91, 92
Vitamin E, 81, 82, 86
Vitamins, 35, 36, 47, 63,
    65, 67, 73, 75, 78-81,
    83, 85, 86, 91-94, 165

## W

Wheat, 35, 37, 38, 48,
    71, 72, 78, 80
Whole-picture, 148
Worry, 27, 113, 128

## Y

Yale University School
    of Medicine, 60

## Z

Zinc, 81-83, 91, 92

# *About the Author*

**Jane Oelke, N.D., Ph.D.,** is a Naturopath and Homeopathic Practitioner in the southwest Michigan area. She works with clients to help them improve their health naturally. She uses Electro-Dermal Screening and Bio-Chemical Nutrition Testing to evaluate health levels and then recommends homeopathic, herbal, and nutritional supplements according to the client's symptoms and test results.

She has worked with adults and children with Attention Deficit Disorder since 1993. She developed the Homeopathic Remedy Chart included in this book and has used it to assist her in determining which homeopathic remedy fits the symptoms of her client.

She has also taught the Brain Exercises in Section 4 in presentations to parent groups and teachers, after using them regularly with her clients.

She is available for presentations and seminars based on the information in this book, and her other book *"Natural Choices for Fibromyalgia."*

She can be contacted through her website at: www.NaturalChoicesForYou.com, or by calling her St. Joseph office toll-free to at 1-888-893-7225